Justin Petrone

Dear Tom!

I hope that this book will make you understand better what kind a people we are :))

U and A.

MISSION ESTONIA
JUSTIN PETRONE
Copyright: Justin Petrone
Editor: Epp Petrone
Copy Editor: Stewart Johnson
Designer: Anneli Akinde
Cover photos: Maiken Staak

Sections of this text have appeared previously
on the blogs *www.justinpetrone.wordpress.com* and
www.palun.blogspot.com, and in the Estonian-language
magazines Anne & Stiil and Eesti Naine.

AS Ajakirjade Kirjastus, 2013
Print: Print Best OÜ
ISBN 978-9949-502-89-9

Mission Estonia
Justin Petrone

Table of Contents

Foreword

Foreword

I found something out of the ordinary the other day. It was a CD insert. Not that it's so uncommon that I find CD inserts, especially when sorting through the mounds of possessions I have managed to accumulate in my short life.

But this insert was different. It was colorful, covered in childlike cartoons, and the text inside bubbled with surrealistic humor. There was so much life in that little sheet of folded paper. And it was unusual because it had my name on it. I was the one who drew those pictures and wrote the text, it said. And I was the one who had made the music on the CD.

My music career! I had forgotten all about it. How I had spent hours in my parents' basement, messing around with guitars and basses and harmonicas and a homemade drum kit I made out of a cardboard box because I couldn't afford a real kit or good drum-programming software. (Cardboard sounds great, by the way.)

Later in London, when I met up with Epp the first time after our trip in Finland, I brought these same CDs and printed out a pile of CD inserts at an acquaintance's apartment. He happened to have a very good printer, because he also specialized in fake passports.

After that I went to the headquarters of my favorite label, Rough Trade Records, in West London, handed a CD to the old British guy in the basement who listens to all the demos. He took it, thanked me and tossed it on to an overflowing pile of other CDs. But I wasn't discouraged. I traveled all over that city by train and bus and foot, through rainy English weather, handing off my disc to different companies, hoping that they would listen to my life's work and make me into a big star so I never had to work a stupid desk job.

It's funny to think that I was once so idealistic that I had a dream. But I did. My dream was to be a musician. I just loved music so much that I had to spend hundreds of dollars making an album over two years in some guy's basement in New York a few years later. We had to pause from time to time because the neighbor made noise when he was lifting weights. All of the insulation the music producer could muster couldn't keep those screeching dumbbells out of his studio.

"I just knew I was going to make it, just knew it," the producer confided in me once as we sat around waiting for the neighbor to stop lifting weights. "I thought I was good enough, but, well, still haven't made it yet."

Making it. We thought that if we were good enough it could happen. Yet luck also had something to do with it, and I didn't seem to have much luck when it came to music (nor did most of the other musicians I played with). I gigged in small clubs in New York City for some time, for free, but as my free time decreased, the gigs became less frequent, and I played the guitar less. We moved to Estonia and I started to do other things in my free time.

Like writing.

I remember how it felt when the first *My Estonia* book came out and I had been invited to discuss it on the morning talk show. A few days later, I walked into a friend's apartment and I saw the heads of all my friends and acquaintances and people I had never met before turn and look in my direction in an intense way and then I went and hid in the bathroom.

As I crouched there beside the toilet a sentence came to mind, "Fame doesn't sit very comfortably on anybody's shoulders, but on some people's shoulders it doesn't seem to fit at all."

That's what Mick Jagger said about Brian Jones, his former Rolling Stones bandmate who drowned at age 27 in a swimming pool while he was under the influence of drugs.

Those men had real fame, the success I had so lusted after as I scurried around their home city handing out my CD to whatever label would accept it. Now I had experienced something similar to it, albeit at a much smaller scale, and it had happened by accident! When the first book came out, I expected it might find the same amount of readers as the other books in the series. I wasn't prepared that it would sell, three, four, five times more than those other books. And I definitely wasn't ready to be accosted by merry drunks yelling out to me from their apartment windows, "Hey Petrone! Good book!"

Good? I'm still not sure if it was that good, but some people liked it. They liked it so much that they wanted more.

So I tried to please them. First I wrote *My Estonia 2*, a more artistic, stream-of-consciousness take on my Estonian life. Some people liked that one. The other was *Montreal Demons*, a travel novel about sex and God. Some people liked that book, too.

But I have a feeling these readers are still not satisfied. They miss that easy humor and the goofy descriptions of local cuisine. Have I tried *sült*, Estonia's delicious jellied meat? Was it as bad as I had imagined? Or have I become a *sült* convert? They want to know.

They are waiting.

"The curse of the second album," said a friend of mine who used to work as a disc jockey. "Bands come in, they record a great album, they make it, then they have to record another one, and it's not as easy, because nobody wants the second album, they want the first album again, and they will never get it."

It then occurred to me that if my handmade demo had been accepted in London all those years ago, and my music had been a hit, I would have probably been in the same position as I am now. It just feels a little bit different than I thought it would in those more idealistic times.

Still, I have to tell you, putting together this new book, *Mission Estonia*, wasn't a headache-inducing experience at all. This wasn't a planned book. Often I wrote these columns to blow off steam while I was on the road traveling to different work conferences around the world, or up late at night knocking out news articles. I didn't write them to satisfy some public desire for another *My Estonia* book, or to prove to myself that I could write an edgy novel. I wrote these columns about Estonia for the pure fun of it. For the first time in a long while, I felt good about doing something artistic. Sometimes I laughed out loud while I was writing. I felt reenergized, like I had regained my voice and found myself again.

It almost makes me want to take another crack at music.

PS. Why hide it? My better-quality recordings are now available online and can be downloaded for free at *www.justinpetrone.com*. I hope you enjoy them!

Look,
It's Him!

It happened the other day on a street in Tartu. Strolling along, I walked past two teenage girls who were glancing in my direction and giggling, to which I greeted them with a wave, but they only giggled more and walked away.

Is something wrong with me? I wondered. *Is my fly undone?* I checked and it wasn't, so I decided to forget about those two girls and I walked to the University Café to buy some chocolate. The November darkness brings on a chocolate craving like you wouldn't believe. I'm like a drug addict. And while I was paying for my fix, I noticed two completely different girls staring at me from a table. "Look," one whispered. "It's him." When I looked in their direction, they also started to giggle. And to make matters worse, an old guy who was reading a newspaper nearby looked me up and down, too, as if he had seen me before. *What the?*

Am I famous? I don't know, or rather, I am beginning to suspect that I might be, at least just a little bit. My life doesn't yet resemble the opening sequence of the first Austin Powers movie, where the International Man of Mystery is chased around a city by screaming girls, but I am beginning to understand what that might feel like.

I first became acquainted with fame Estonian style thanks to my wife, Epp. She hasn't done anything that unusual—she's written a few books and magazine columns—but a lot of people seem to know who she is. For years now I have walked by store windows seeing her name in print from behind the glass, "Epp Petrone". I've seen magazine interviews and newspaper articles about her. When our second daughter was born, it warranted a newspaper headline. I've even noticed people staring at us on the street from time to time, though mostly in her direction.

Still, I didn't come to know that special "Austin Powers" feeling until recently. It's a new challenge for me, of navigating the line between what is personal and what is public, and this probably doesn't just affect the so-called famous, but anybody who chooses to share their personal lives on a blog or social network, so that you introduce yourself to strangers at parties and they tell you not to bother because they already know all there is to know about you.

I've come to wonder, what is the difference between being famous and not famous? In New York, from where I come, it's not just a matter of being on TV or on the cover of a newspaper or magazine. No, the celebrities live an entirely different lifestyle. They don't fly commercial, they take private jets. They don't eat at the corner restaurant, they dine at exclusive clubs. They don't suntan at the public beach, they tan at their own estates. There is a huge gulf between the famous and the average. If you are lucky enough to actually see one of these famous people in person, you might tell all your friends at the office.

In Estonia, it's different. Here, the well-known man and common man do almost everything together. They both do their shopping at the local department store. They both take the same package trips to the same exotic destinations. I've been told that Estonia is such a small country that there is a very thin line between being well known and unknown, and I think it's true. Estonians rub elbows with public figures all the time. You go to the store in Tallinn, and a quarter of the parliament might be in there picking up groceries. That's just how it is.

But while the relationship between so-called celebrities and non-celebrities in Estonia is different from the US, the channels through which celebrities are made are the same. How did people figure out who I was to begin with? They saw me on television or heard me on the radio or read about me in a magazine or newspaper article. And after several TV appearances and radio interviews, the local taxi driver is looking in the rear view mirror and saying, "Hey, you're the guy who wrote that book."

How to react to this newfound awareness of my existence? I've tried to think about it, but I keep failing to settle on any profound thought to guide me through scenarios where diners at a café drop their forks and start laughing when they see me at the cash register. I'm told that experienced celebrities tip their hat or smile or even go and introduce themselves. I'm not there yet. In the University Café in Tartu, I grabbed my chocolate, turned, and ran with the sounds of giggling girls in my ears (and checked my zipper again, just to be sure).

Anyway, I've come to see celebrities in a new light. They really are just people like you or me. And I have decided something. If I ever meet someone genuinely famous, I'll make sure not to burst into laughter or give them a weird look or chase them down the street seeking an autograph. Instead, I'll just let them go on their way.

Estonian Men and Foreign Men

Every Estonian word I learn has its origin. It was from watching Urmas Ott interview Tallinn Mayor Edgar Savisaar that I first heard the word *arvamus* ("opinion"). And it was the writer Andrus Kivirähk who blessed my vocabulary with the words *tallalakkuja* ("bootlicker"), *lipitseja* ("brown noser"), and *porihing* ("dirt soul").

My vocabulary is expanding constantly, and when the cover of the tabloid *Õhtuleht* greeted me the other day with the headline: *Eesti mehed on jobud?* ("Are Estonian men *jobud*?") I understood it. Estonian manhood does seem to be going through some kind of crisis and the word *jobu (pronounced "yo-boo," plural jobud)* encapsulates what Estonian men see as wrong with themselves. I have even heard there is a *Jobu* magazine in development. But what does the word even mean?

I'm pretty sure it was Epp who taught me the word

jobu, though I can't remember which *jobu* she was talking about at the time. At first I thought *jobu* meant a drunk, because the most commonly used word for drunk is *joodik*, and *jobu* and *joodik* sound a little similar. But, as I have learned, a *jobu* is not merely a drunk. A *jobu* is something different, something more profound. My favorite online English–Estonian dictionary equates *jobu* with the following terms: birdbrain, blithering idiot, bumpkin, daft, jerk, prat, turkey, and zombie(!). Is this really how Estonian men see themselves?

It gets worse. From the articles I have read, the archenemy of all *jobud* is the foreign man—in other words, me. The foreign man is everything the Estonian man is not: allegedly wealthy, supposedly slick—a smooth operator. In one recent column, the Estonian man actually went so far as to give up smoking so that he could compete with the foreign man, because the foreign man doesn't smoke. I actually find this soul searching necessary, because if the specter of the foreign man can get some Estonian guys to eat right and quit smoking, if their foreign foe can get the average male's life expectancy to inch over 70 years, then I'm happy to play the villain. Competition is good.

Still, there are critiques I hear from *jobud* that are troublesome. One is that by marrying foreigners, Estonian women are somehow betraying their country. There are so few Estonians, this argument goes. Estonians need to make more of them, together, in Estonia. By partnering with a foreigner, the pure bloodstream of the Estonians is tainted, polluted. The future of the nation is flushed down the toilet the second that foreign sperm connects with Estonian egg.

This is not true. Biological diversity should be welcomed, not shunned. National homogeneity is wonderful if you want to study rare genetic diseases, but it's not going to make your population any more flexible or open to the world. And the tragedy of the slow death of the "pure" Estonian at the hands of swashbuckling foreigners is that, as political scientist Rein Taagepera describes the local attitude, "There are only two real Estonians in Estonia, me and you, and I'm not so sure about you." Scratch an Estonian and you're bound to find some other nationality. I've even heard that there is an abundance of brunettes on Saaremaa because some Portuguese pirates once went on a spree. The well was contaminated long before I showed up.

And not only by foreign men. I have met plenty of women in my travels, women that were once desperate and lonesome, that is, until the day that some guy named Uno or Raivo walked into their lives. I've met Americans, Brits, Swedes, Finns, Russians—all of whom just couldn't resist the temptation of the Estonian man. And, for some reason, Estonian women don't resent these foreign women for choosing an Estonian husband. The lecturing only goes one way.

It's a shame that *jobud* detest the foreign man. They don't understand their strengths. One can only imagine the sharp pangs of shame the foreign man feels when his Estonian partner discovers that, unlike most Estonian men, he doesn't know how to build his own house. Or so it seems. Because as the time a foreign man spends in Estonia increases, the probability of him becoming involved in a grueling construction project approaches 1. By that point, when he's sweaty and covered in sawdust and paint and pauses to seek some relief in a beer after a hot day of work in the countryside, it doesn't really matter if he's local or foreign. He's bound to look like a *jobu* anyway.

What Should
I Do with My Hair?

This is what she's been asking me for days now, she being Epp, my wife of nearly ten years. It really sounds like a stupid question, doesn't it, the answer to which can only be, "Do whatever you feel like." That's what I usually tell her at first, but we both know it's not good enough.

When I met her she had a huge mane of curly dirty blonde locks and she looked like a lion. I was fixated on it, I just kept looking at the jungle bush growing on her head, it fired me up and lured me in. Over the years, the wilderness has been tamed and domesticated. It's been long, medium, and short, straight and curled, bangs, no bangs, brown, blonde, red, pink.

Through most of the experimentation, I've encouraged her to find her way on her own. "What do you think? Listen to yourself." The problem is in the listening. Sometimes the voice is faint. Other times there are too many voices. And all the time the hair appointment time is approaching. It cannot be postponed again. The drama builds. "What should I do with my hair? What do you think I should do?"

In these situations, I usually suggest a reversion to natural. Why not? I imagine that it is easier to maintain your own hair color over time. No need for special shampoos to maintain an artificial color. But the dilemma for a lot of women seems to be that they left their natural hair color behind in their teens, and they aren't quite sure what it is anymore. It's a question for historians. There is the photographic evidence; a few scattered memoirs have been collected. Pieced together it is something, but, the pensive historians warn us, don't expect any kind of historical truth. It doesn't exist!

Her childhood photos reveal a small pygmy with a crown of yellow, but somewhere around adolescence, the dark set in, a color common to Estonians, known as "potato brown." It was the last time nature ruled. After that came the dyeing, the experimenting; the "disco haircut" that left her looking a little too much like one of the guys in Duran Duran; the flowing perms that earned her the college nickname "Koidula". Like a tormented actor, her hair has been through so many incarnations, it's lost its true sense of self. "Who the hell am I?" it seems to cry in the mirror. And there is no turning back. Is there?

When it comes to hair, all I see around me are visual lies. My mother continues to insist that she is natural blonde, but I remember her roots used to be dark before the gray set in. But one cannot argue with it. Natural blonde! It's the official policy. My grandmother was a boisterous Irish red until one day her hair turned tundra white. When I asked my mother how Grandma had aged so fast, almost overnight, she said that Grandma had simply been dyeing it red before she started dyeing it white. So Grandma wasn't really red *or* white. She was something else, something that nobody knew. What is Grandma's true hair color? It's a question for Egyptologists.

So there is no going back. But what is the way forward? The appointment at the salon looms. The minutes are ticking away. The situation calls for decisiveness. "What should I do with my hair?" she asks again. Why does she always ask me? Does she really want to know? Do women really expect their men to say, "Listen honey, I want it wavy and shoulder-length this time, with blonde highlights," like they were ordering a dish at a restaurant? Wouldn't any man who responded like that warrant a good smack in the face with a woman's magazine? Maybe a spritz in the eyes with some detangling spray?

"Never interfere when it comes to a woman and her hair," I have been advised. It's the eleventh commandment and I agree. Who wants to take the blame for a salon catastrophe? But what about equality? My wife makes suggestions to me all the time and I listen intently, because to men, women really are like civilization in the flesh. If it weren't for the women in our lives, most of us would probably never change our socks.

But here is the difference: women are more nuanced in their approach. She won't tell you that you should change your socks outright, no, she might just happen to buy you some more and wash them. "They were on sale," she'll say, "And look, they are just your size!" Likewise, she won't tell you she prefers your hair long, she'll just happen to run her fingers through it and say, "Mmm, you look good today." That way, when we men go to get a haircut, there is no question about what we should do with our hair.

Long Distance
Families

A neighbor of ours has a child, but this child lives in New Zealand, which is very far away. It's so far away that I don't know the name of our neighbor's child, or if it is male or female. I don't want to ask, because our neighbor looked so sad when I asked if she had any children.

New Zealand really is at the edge of the Earth. Sometimes, I tell my mother that while Estonia might seem like a long way from New York, it's actually kind of close. "It could be worse," I say. "We could live in New Zealand."

That never seems to make her feel better. She has resigned herself to a life of misery and longing over what might have been if I had never left my home-town. She's tired of talking to my children via Skype, and being a "virtual" grandmother, she says. She commiserates with the neighbor across the street, whose daughter lives in the Netherlands. They both long for the good old days, when families were close, both physically and emotionally.

But is ours really the first generation to suffer from the malady of globalization? I don't think so. I think that in the past, it was even harder. Think of my poor great grandmother Maria who left the sunny fields of Bari in southern Italy for the frigid winters of New York. And she never went back! Not once in her life. As an old woman, she sat, staring at the window and sighing to herself, perhaps thinking of Italy. At least, that's what I have been told.

In comparison, the ease with which we travel these days is a true luxury. In the nearly 50 years that she spent in New York, Maria never went back once to Italy. But our friend Airi comes to visit Estonia from her adopted home in Australia at least once a year. These are action-packed visits too. Airi stayed about a day and a half at our house, where we drank wine and watched a movie. Then she was off to Tallinn, with plans to go to Riga the day after that. She has so many people to see in those two weeks that she is here. And my visits to the US are the same, brief encounters with friends and relatives, and then back onto the big airplane.

In my meetings with readers, I have met many sad-eyed grandmothers who bought books to send to their children in California or Australia or Brazil. Sometimes, I get the sense it's to "show" their children that not everybody leaves Estonia for love. They have the same miserable look in their eye as my mother. It's a look that shows that God has cheated them by denying them the right to have grandkids that live on the same street. And as much as they might think the weather in California is wonderful, inside they hate California for stealing their baby. They long to have all of their relatives dwelling within a short driving distance.

The funny thing is that many of Epp's relatives actually do live within driving distance, some even within walking distance, and we don't see them so often. Grandma in the countryside gets one or two visits per season. Even my sister-in-law, who lives 10 minutes away, can disappear from our lives for weeks on end. If I added up all the days I have spent with my American family in the past five years and all the days I have spent with my Estonian family, they would probably be about even, if not tilted toward the Americans, with those month-long summer or winter visits. So much for living so far away!

That's still no consolation for those who miss their closest relatives. They are still unhappy. I have spent a lot of time trying to figure out why it is that some people roam so far from the nest. After all that meditation, I have come to the conclusion that some people simply must leave home. Should Barack Obama have stayed in Honolulu? Should Toomas Hendrik Ilves have stayed in Leonia, New Jersey? Should Kerli Kõiv have never strayed from the city limits of Elva? I have an American friend in Estonia who used to work in a warehouse in the US. Now he's the CEO of an important company and spends his days jetting around from Nigeria to Japan to Brazil. "Sometimes you just have to take risks," he says of his life. And that means that some of us have to leave home. It's hard on families, sure, it will break a mother's heart, but, as I pointed out, physical distance and emotional distance are not always correlated.

Plus, as much as the sight of a big, extended family might make a person whose child lives in New Zealand jealous, the dirty truth is that a lot of these family members can barely tolerate each other. I know one Estonian woman who lived with her family for years in the US before returning home. I asked her recently if she ever thought of moving back. I thought she would say "no," because it's so swell to be in Estonia, but she confided in me that she actually misses America a great deal.

"We were so free there, we could do whatever we pleased," she told me. "And you know," she glanced over her shoulder, "in America we didn't have so many relatives around!"

Mr. Antonovka

Estonian months carry a variety of alternate names. Glance at a calendar and you will see that July or *Juuli* is also referred to as *heinakuu*—"hay month"—a month where, I gather, you are supposed to make a lot of hay.

Oktoober's alter ego is *viinakuu*—"vodka month"— named so because of people's fondness for vodka-making. If I were the one printing calendars, though, I would give October a different name, *õunakuu*—"apple month"—because it's the month when people are busy trying to think of creative ways to get rid of the avalanches of apples in their backyards.

Estonians treat apples more kindly than they treat one another. Harvesting begins not with ascending a ladder to pluck nature's bounty from your personal orchard, but with searching the ground for apples that have dropped overnight that might still be good. Good apples are never wasted. Even the bruised ones can be sliced and made into jams or used in cakes.

Only after you have personally judged the quality of every grounded apple can you move to the trees. Using both methods, we collected about eight bags of fruit recently, resulting in liters and liters and liters of apple juice. We also have jars and jars and jars of sweet apple jam. But the apples kept coming. The following weekend, I scavenged, picked, and cleaned four more bags of fruit. A group of Estonian guys up in the Tartu neighborhood of Veeriku works round the clock making juice for Tartu residents for a fee. For 180 kroons our apples were turned to raw juice overnight. We boiled the juice and packed away even more jars of the stuff for the months to come. But there were still more apples! So this weekend I picked six more bags and brought it to the Veeriku juice factory. This time, though, I went without my spouse.

The leader of the Veeriku gang is a guy who looks to be in his 50s or 60s. He wears an old sweater, and has a salt-and-pepper beard and a ruddy face that looks like he's seen too many saunas. He also suffers from southern Estonian mud tongue—that is, he sort of mumbles in a deep voice. Only other Estonians can truly understand the system of grunts and sighs that make up this variety of the language. I managed to make it through most of the conversation. Then he pointed at my apples and said something about "Antonovka". I figured that he thought my name was Antonovka—that I was an Estonian Russian. I do have a noticeable accent.

"No, my name is not Antonovka," I told him.

"No, no, these apples, are they Antonovka's?" he grunted.

"No, they're our apples, not Antonovka's."

"I know they are your apples. But what kind of apples are they?"

Now, I attended preschool in the United States, so I know the names of different apples. The big yellow ones are called Yellow Delicious. The big red ones are called Red Delicious. And the tart green ones: Granny Smith. How would I translate "Granny Smith" into Estonian, I ponder? *Vanaema Sepp*? But the reality is that none of our apples look like those American apples. The ones here are all a little different.

"Well, some of our apples are red and some are yellow," I told the Veeriku juice-maker. "Those are the kinds of apples we have."

He sighed and took down my number, but I gave him Epp's name, because I didn't even want to go through the process of spelling out my name or, even worse, being reminded that I share a name with American pop singer Justin Timberlake.

I asked Epp about Mr. Antonovka when I got home, but she just laughed, and told me that Antonovkas are a kind of apple. There is no Mr. Antonovka. My mistake! Later, when I brought my daughter to visit a friend, I discussed the dilemma of Estonia's over productive apple orchards with her father. Margus was standing at the top of the driveway, twisting the top of a juice press. Beside him was one large wheelbarrow filled with apple pulp, another tub filled with raw juice, and then two more plastic tubs filled with apples.

"I've been drinking apple juice for weeks," he said proudly. "I won't need to buy juice from the store all winter."

I related my tale to Margus. "I went to get the juice pressed in Veeriku, and the man kept asking me about Antonovka—I thought he thought it was my name!"

Margus laughed. "There are lots of different kinds of apples in Estonia that you probably don't have in America. Antonovka apples come originally from Russia. They don't taste so great, but they last a long time."

I realized he was right. They probably don't have *Vanaema Sepp* apples in Estonia. And I haven't seen any Yellow Delicious at the store. I'm still a foreigner in a foreign country. It's like John Travolta's character says in *Pulp Fiction*. The funniest thing about Europe is the little differences. "I mean they got the same shit over there that they got here," he tells Samuel L. Jackson's character, "but it's just there it's a little different."

But it doesn't end with the raw juice, because the juice has to be boiled and jarred, and that can cause all kinds of logistical headaches. When is the right time to begin boiling? Who will be on straining duty to skim off all the nasty foam that rises to the top? And worst of all, what do we do when we run out of jars?

You'd think the answer to the last question is just to head to the store. There are always more jars, right? This is a capitalist country. There is supply and demand. If the people demand jars then the stores will order more. Sure, Estonia is on the east coast of the Baltic Sea, but it's not the middle of nowhere, is it? Such simple things as jars must be as plentiful as, well, as plentiful as apples in a Tartu backyard.

I am sorry to report that there were no more jars at the Zeppelin shopping center in Tartu. Nor were there any at Eedeni Keskus. The Rimi Hypermarket was also out. And Selver didn't have any either.

Kas teil purke on? (Do you have any more jars?) We asked the sellers.

Enam ei ole. (Not any more) They replied.

Enam ei ole. Enam ei ole. I heard that line so many times. How could it be? This is a city of 100,000 people. There must be jars in it, somewhere. As we found out there are, just not at the stores. After searching around, friends began to volunteer huge bags full of empty containers. Apparently, there are ladies all around town that have jars stashed in their cellars. They have more containers than they can fill with fruit byproducts. And the best part of this social networking experience was that we got all our jars for free, though I did spend 51 kroons to buy 30 jar lids. And even after boiling juice by the gallons, there was still one more giant aluminum canister to work through.

"Don't worry," our friend Pille told me. "If you run out of jars, my neighbor has plenty."

"How much apple juice do you drink?" I asked.

"I average about a half liter per day," she said.

And maybe I do, too. I must confess, when I'm in the mood for something quick, I might just grab a jar of juice, a jar of chunky apple jam, and a spoon. They say an apple a day keeps the doctor away. But what about 40 apples? Am I adding years to my life?

As I write this, the sunny morning has given way to a gray, windy noon. The only bits of light that catch my eye from the second floor window are the golden orbs that are suspended before me—the highest-hanging fruit of our personal orchard. It almost makes me sick to look at them. I feel guilty for not making use of every last apple. But there's only so much juice and jam a family in Tartu can make.

The Good
Old Days

The word *aitüma* entered my vocabulary at some point in the recent past. I don't know when and I honestly have no idea what the etymological difference is between *aitüma* and *aitäh* because as far as I can tell they mean the same exact thing, "thank you."

So I started saying it to everyone, to the cashiers in Tallinn and the telemarketers trying to sell me cookbooks and the mailman who delivered my boots. They didn't seem to mind but a few were amused to see this foreign guy standing before them saying that archaic word.

My guess was that *aitüma* was just another funky Southern Estonian dialect word making a comeback. I asked my friend Silver about this and he explained that I was only half right. "Only *ökoinimesed* say *aitüma*," Silver said. "Why?" I asked. "Because it's so cool and old," he said, "and *ökoinimesed* love anything that is old." (*Ökoinimesed* translating as "ecopeople," people who wear old-fashioned clothes and eat only organic foods, people like a lot of our friends and, quite often, like us.)

I liked this dialogue with Silver because it was the first time that someone in my group of friends had been ironic about the popularity of anything aged among the young people of Estonia. But it's true. Call it the *öko* lifestyle or just retro infatuation, the adults around me seem obsessed with traditional life. *Öko* in this sense is nothing new, but rather old, *öko* is the food your grandmother's grandmother ate, *öko* is the clothes your grandmother's grandmother wore. In Viljandi, they advertise dance nights at the *Pärimusmuusika Ait* (the happening Folk Music Center) with images of men and women who look like they could be characters at a wedding from a hundred years ago with their old caps and whiskers and braids and granny dresses.

Mind you, not just anything ancient will do. No one is trying to harken back to the days of the Black Plague or the Napoleonic Wars. Instead, Estonians have settled on an optimal period of nostalgia centered on the 1920s. I hypothesize that this makes life more convenient because the Estonians of the 1920s lived in a sort of limbo between the archaic and modern eras. That is to say that they lived in wooden houses and spoke their various local dialects and largely ate food that they grew on their own and had homespun clothing and milled around drinking homebrewed beers and moonshine, but they also had radios and cars and bicycles and tennis rackets and went swimming in Pärnu and sometimes even holidayed outside of the country. And I think this is what these *öko* people are aiming for: the 1920s plus wireless Internet, for the Internet is the one modern thing that *öko* people will never abandon.

There is a deep irony here. To hear old-timers tell it, nobody wanted to live in the dark, crooked old wooden houses of Kalamaja in Tallinn or Karlova in Tartu in the 1950s and 1960s. Back then people dreamed of a life beyond their ramshackle old neighborhoods, of obtaining an apartment in modern housing projects like Tallinn's Mustamäe district or Tartu's Annelinn, a comfortable existence of organized building maintenance and central heating, of vacuum cleaners to pick up dust and gas-heated stoves to do the cooking, and, with all that leisure time, a proper television to entertain a family into the late hours.

Today, their grandchildren boast about the virtues of wood-heated furnaces, think the crooked old wooden houses are charming, clean the house with brooms and wet rags, gave the TV away long ago, and cook carrots and potatoes or porridges or bread in the fireplace. And it's the pensioners, the very people who were the little children during this vaunted golden age and the only ones who actually remember it, who are now living alone in the apartment blocks of Estonia with their eyes glued to Latin soap operas, eating canned meats and vegetables and factory-made bread.

This has led me to wonder—will any of our current creature comforts become fashionable in the same way,

50 or 100 years from now? Maybe our grandchildren will astonish us by trying to imitate life as my generation lived it as children in the 1980s, with no Internet (because there was no Internet), no mobile phones (because there were no mobile phones), no piercings or tattoos (because only junkie guitarists had tattoos), no GPS (only foldable paper roadmaps), and no bicycle helmets (because nobody wore bike helmets back then). Some might argue that this has already happened. As my friend Hannes, a former music label owner, informed me, nobody wants to buy CDs anymore, but vinyl is making a comeback. I haven't relied on vinyl for music since I was eight years old, but chances are I will be playing records again.

Or maybe the 1980s will be forgotten, and it is the 2000s we will aspire to recreate, the "good old days" when people had laptops for computing, mobile phones for calling, and iPods for listening to music, not just one high-tech instrument for doing all of these things. In Estonia, future generations may yearn for "good old" *euroremont*, ah, those vinyl floors, those Styrofoam ceilings, those plastic windows, "just like in grandma and grandpa's apartment." Or maybe they will scour the Internet looking for "vintage" versions of programs like Skype, not the modern one, but the first version, just so they can feel like an earlier, more idealistic, more genuine denizen of the web.

If such things do come to pass, I am sure they will elicit a few chuckles from old geezers like us, and maybe more than a little *déjà vu*.

In Soviet
Times

The turn of phrase "in Soviet times" is often heard among Estonians, especially among a certain age group, the ones in their 30s and 40s who are old enough to remember the "Soviet times" but were not old enough to partake in them beyond singing carols to Lenin in school or having their photo taken next to the "Soldier–Liberator" in central Tallinn.

Though the memories of those days are fading, I have heard here in Estonia that all sorts of things can still be attributed to the "Soviet times". For example, why are people so quiet on public transportation? Supposedly, it is because people were intimidated by the Soviet security apparatus. They were everywhere, listening to everything, even on trams! That's why people are so quiet.

These same Estonians dare not mention that in Copenhagen, Oslo and Helsinki the passengers are just as silent. Northern Europeans, I have found, are generally quiet on trams. It has nothing to do with "Soviet times".

Or how come Estonian students don't raise their hands in the classroom? I was told this is also due to the "Soviet times", a strange era when the best students were the ones who asked the fewest questions. But the students in my classes aren't all from former Soviet countries. The Norwegians and Finns in class don't talk much either.

My favorite "in Soviet times" stories revolve around totally pointless things that have no bearing on modern life. I was once told by two women, both about 40, that "today is Thursday and *in Soviet times* we would be having fish!" Do I look like I care what food you ate on Thursdays 30 years ago?

But for the sake of nostalgia, I thought I'd share with you an "in Soviet times" story. In Soviet times, there was a student in my school named Igor. Like so many students he was one of those lucky people who managed to escape from a communist country to the glorious glitz of the West. In my school there were Croatians and Poles and Rumanians and, yes, Russians like Igor, you see. They had pulled all kinds of strings to get out of their home countries and we welcomed them with open arms.

However, there was some acrimony and it was in the heady days of the late 1980s that the Cold War finally made its way into scholastic discourse. And one way it manifested itself was by yelling terrible things at Igor about his collapsing country.

I can still recall sitting on the bus and several bus windows being lowered as poor Igor stood on the sidewalk near the school waiting for his bus. From the windows was put forward the kind of language one wouldn't expect from an old sailor, let alone a class of 12-year-olds. Something to the tune of "Up Yours, You Goddamn Commie!"

To which Igor indulged us by thrusting his middle finger up in the air and yelling back—forgive me— "Fuck you, you stupid, capitalist pig American fucks, fuck you!"

As you can tell, Igor was already proficient in the English language. He also had that hysterical accent that almost no Russian can lose, no matter what language they speak. So all the kids on the bus absolutely loved to tease Igor, just so we could listen to him say our swear words in his funny Slavic way.

And that is sort of what I remember most about those days. Nobody hated Igor because he came from the Soviet Union. Instead, we loved to pretend that we hated Igor. Likewise, Igor probably didn't hate us. He liked to pretend that he hated us.

To tell you the truth, that's the first time I have thought about Igor in decades. I wonder what he's up to now. I hope Igor is happy, no matter where he may be, and he's not bugging some stranger in, say, California, with tales of Thursday night fish fries during his cozy, Soviet childhood, the days before he moved to the land of the capitalist pigs.

So why do we continue to elevate this period in our consciences? I have a theory it's because the change from "Soviet times" to "modern times" (I prefer to call them "European times" because of EU accession) was so abrupt.

In the span of a few years, the Soviet state and everything that supported it was dismantled and replaced with the recycled beliefs of the Estonian Republic of yore or ideas stolen from some other land in order to make the country as European as possible in the shortest amount of time.

Because of this, the Soviet era has become something of legend, a mythical time like the age of King Arthur that few would really believe in if there weren't the heaps of television footage and old newspapers lying around. All that's really left are some crumbling buildings, some old monuments, and middle-aged ladies talking about fish Thursdays. I've come to think that, for them, talking about "Soviet times" is probably less about warm nostalgia for the past, and more about coping with a lifetime of change.

Facebook
"Friends"

Last week, I found out that an old girlfriend of mine is expecting a baby. She's 20 weeks along, and the ultrasound revealed another joy-inducing fact: it's a girl. When she shared this information with me, I was overwhelmed with positive feelings. After all that had happened between us, all of that acrimony, we could both be looking forward to a happier future.

Oh, there's one thing I forgot to add. My ex didn't tell me in person that she was pregnant. No, she told me and the rest of the world via Facebook.

The sad truth is that I denied her friendship requests two times on the world's most popular social networking site. Why? Maybe I just didn't want to share everything with her. But in the end, I decided that I had nothing big to hide and accepted her request. And why the hell not? I'm now "friends" with dozens of people I went to high school with that I barely knew at the time. I'm even "friends" with Estonian politicians Mart Laar and Marko Mihkelson. And if I am going to be "friends" with Estonian politicians, I might as well be "friends" with my ex-girlfriend.

I have to admit that at first I was kind of excited to have such immediate access to her life. Whatever happened between us, I still cared about her, and I was excited to be able to see what she looked like and what she was up to and if she was dating. And the best part of it all was that I was able to see all that stuff without having to go through the trouble of actually communicating with her! It seems terrible, doesn't it? But when I think about this odd online relationship, though, I wonder about all the "friends" out there who are using me the exact same way. It's mutual voyeurism, and the truth is that I am not really sure how it started.

OK, I remember now. I was being driven over the San Francisco Bay Bridge on the way to the airport after a work-related conference. It was a sunny day, and I was looking out the window at the bay. As she drove, my real-life friend (they still exist) was telling me about how she met her husband while he was engaged to someone else, and how he left his fiancé for her, and how his ex hated her until the ex got married and had a baby and now it's all water under the bridge because they are all "friends" on Facebook. And my friend told me that I should join Facebook, too, because you could post photos and updates and keep in touch with old friends, like her. And so, as soon as I got back to Estonia, I started a Facebook account.

That's how it started. Like any good sheep I followed the herd and began sharing my personal information, joining groups to which I had some affinity (Petrones of the World, Fans of Lennart Meri, etc.), and, before I knew it, I had befriended dozens of people whom I didn't really consider to be "friends", but didn't have the heart to deny a friendship request. And in the mix of throngs of new "friends" I let through the gates were people like my ex-girlfriend, the ghosts of the past, the people you wonder about in those fleeting moments while you are filling up your gas tank or buying cat food at the store. The people who can still make you feel a little vulnerable, even if you haven't seen them in years.

Goddamn you Facebook! From time to time, I've thought of destroying it all and deleting my account. My wife, who has also joined Facebook, dismisses such thoughts as "social suicide". And why would I want to end my online social networking life, when I can read all my "real friends'" funny daily updates or see new photos of their adventures in exotic countries? As in all things, there is a balance between positives and negatives. For every person you don't know so well, there is a charming real friend you haven't seen in years because he or she lives far away, and only via Facebook can you keep in daily contact. There's good and there's bad and you can't only have good, can you?

My wife has befriended a number of ex-boyfriends, too, via Facebook, and I am not sure how I should feel about that either. Should I worry? Should I not notice? Is it all for fun or is there something else going on? Oh well. I guess the only thing I can really do is "friend" them, too.

Love Is All
You Need

"All you need is love, love, love is all you need." So The Beatles sang over a full orchestra in 1967 and so their words of love reached my young ears twenty years later. I was my elementary school's youngest Beatles fan. While other kids amused themselves with video games, I had inherited my parents' record collection and I would stay up late at night watching the old vinyl spin round, trying to decipher what exactly this "love" thing meant that the Fab Four were always singing about.

Whatever love was, it sounded like something I needed. From the adrenaline rush I got every time I listened to the rocking "She Loves You"—yeah, yeah, yeah—to the cool calm that would set in whenever I heard the harmonica on "Love Me Do", to the jingle jangle of "Can't Buy Me Love", I was hooked on love. I just had to have this wonderful thing. So I set my sights on a girl in the grade above me. She was an unusual choice, very dark hair, porcelain skin, round face, mysterious brown eyes; she could have been Japanese if she wasn't Jewish. I don't think any other little boys were in love with her, but I was sure that I was in love with her, so I began to write her letters, passed by my courier, a classmate who rode the same bus with the little mysterious girl.

My friend did warn me that this girl was mean. "She once hit me over the head with a chessboard," he said. "I hate her." This should have turned me off, but it just made her that much more intriguing. "Who is this girl who hits boys?" I wondered. "What is her secret?"

I knew she was absolutely the one for me and so I wrote to her, though most of the words in my love letters were copied from Beatles songs. "Love, love me do," I wrote her. "I'll always be true." At the end, I added, of course, "PS. I love you." I waited anxiously for her response, but when it finally came, I was shattered. "Stop writing me these stupid letters," she cursed me. "You are ugly and I hate your guts."

I was crushed by her rejection. I cried in my room all night. If love was so great that The Beatles sang about it all the time, then how come it hurt so much? But her letter didn't dissuade me. No. Instead I fell more deeply in love with her and wrote her even more, to which she replied with more terse, offensive responses. By the end of the year I was heartbroken and decided that it was probably time to find another girl to fall in love with. It was only later I found out that my classmate never passed the letters to her. He had been writing her nasty responses all by himself, the little bastard! He really did deserve to get hit over the head with a chessboard! It was the end of our short-lived friendship.

Anyway, I did find another girl to fall in love with. And one after that. And one after that. And after a long time, my idea of love began to change and I thought I'd started to understand it a little better. One could now say that I have gained wisdom in all my years of love, wisdom that could be shared, wisdom that could be passed down to the younger generation. Or maybe not. Because these days I see my daughter is reliving my elementary school experiences.

It's not The Beatles that are informing her pursuit for love, though. This time it's 2009 Eurovision winner Alexander Rybak. "I'm in love with a fairytale, even though it hurts," the Belarusian-Norwegian croons, leaping around with fiddle in hand. "I don't care if I lose my mind, I'm already cursed." My daughter loves that song. She watches it over and over again on YouTube. I can see that it hurts her a bit to watch it, to be in love with someone like Alexander, somebody so unattainable, a man whom she can only view through a tiny clip on the Internet. That bittersweet feeling. I remember it so well from my school days.

But there is another side to this story. In my daughter's school, there is a little boy—let's call him Martin—who has fallen deeply in love. With my daughter. I can see it in his words and deeds. My absent-minded daughter will forget her backpack in the classroom and then use him. "Martin, go and bring me my backpack!" And I will stand there and watch as little Martin jogs up the stairs and returns, with red ears, to hand my daughter her bag to which she replies, "Now go away, Martin. I don't want to talk to you anymore today."

I want to interfere, to step in, to teach my daughter that she shouldn't be so obsessed with Alexander and be kinder to Martin. And I want to advise Martin that he should probably find somebody else to fall in love with. But I don't. I just have to stand there and watch them, because there's nothing I can do. These kids will have to learn their own lessons in love.

Jealous Guy

Of all places, we ended the night at the Estonian House on 34th Street. It was Epp's first time in New York, a few days before Christmas 2002, and I was showing her around. We had spent the day together, but at the Estonian House, Epp seemed to lose all interest in me. Instead, my wife-to-be had found a place at the bar next to some older, handsome, golden-haired Estonian journalist. The two sat huddled over their beers, apparently telling each other the most intimate details of their lives. And I sat in the corner and waited for their conversation to end. And waited. And waited. He kept smiling at her. She kept laughing at his jokes. I meantime sipped my beer in the corner and began plotting his murder.

Linda kept me company. She was the daughter of Estonian exiles and spoke a wild mix of English and Estonian, even to people who didn't know any Estonian.

"Do you feel all right?" Linda asked me as I shot angry glances at Epp and her new best friend.

"What do you mean?"

"You were happy when you came in," Linda said. "Now you just look miserable."

"Miserable?" I stole another look at the bar. I could grab one of those heavy liquor bottles, I determined. Then bring it down on his big blonde head.

"Oh my God," Linda put her hand over her mouth as she watched me. "You actually think?" She blushed. "You must really like her. But listen, *kallis*, you don't have anything to worry about," she reached out and touched my hand. "He's not interested in her."

"How do you know?"

"Because he's gay."

"He's gay?" I lowered my face into my hands, rubbing my tired eyes. "You know, Linda, only I could be jealous of a gay guy."

It was true. Jealousy was an emotion I knew well. It had haunted me throughout every relationship, often poisoning the trust between me and the women in my life. I was unsure of its roots, but it had always been there, silently stinging me. And the worst part was that I had no power over my jealousy. It was its own beast. I thought I couldn't control it.

Who were these men of whom I was jealous? In my mind, they were always greater than me. Perhaps they were more outgoing, or more adventurous, or more entertaining, or more successful. The journalist that night at the bar was better dressed, wealthier, older, not to mention Estonian. And who was I? I could rip myself apart in myriad ways. I was moody, clumsy, a big clunky Italian moose. Somehow I could even manage to criticize myself for being jealous.

What I have discovered through years of dealing with this black emotion is that jealousy is not really about the other person, no matter how wonderful it feels to hate them, no matter how titillating it is to plot your revenge. It's actually about your own self worth, the nagging suspicion that you don't deserve your partner, that you are unworthy of her love, and that she must have been a total idiot to wind up with a guy like you.

I know how it feels to have a jealous lover. My wife fortunately is not the jealous type, but I've been with girls who suspected that every random female in my life was a rival. I rarely had seen these mere acquaintances as potential love interests, but, here's the intriguing part, by accusing me of having feelings for another person, I often wound up feeling closer to that other person than to my jealous lover. Jealousy destroys trust between people. You begin to think that maybe that someone else might understand you better than your partner does because you feel less constrained and free to communicate with them.

So what's the solution? How do you kill jealousy?

What I have learned is that you've got to turn the tables on your emotions; rather than tearing yourself down you've got to build yourself up. So what if those guys are more outgoing? You are more insightful. So what if they are older? You are younger. So what if these handsome rivals have pretty northern European features? You have a big beautiful Mediterranean face. No matter how tough it may seem, I believe that a person's will power can be stronger than any negative emotion. Jealousy does sting, but it is always possible to sting it back.

What He
Doesn't Know

When it comes to a woman's past, is don't ask, don't tell really the best policy? I ask this because it seems to be the most favored. Some women think that if they don't tell their partners about their previous affairs, they can avoid the toxic jealousy and emotional fallout that will result when their loved ones learn of the long list of suitors who called before them.

This reminds me of an old friend who for some reason took me as a confidant and liked to inform me of all of her sordid liaisons. Like her fling with that Colombian drug dealer Pablo. Don't ask me how they met but they did and after that, it was just Pablo, Pablo, Pablo. That's all I heard about. There was so much Pablo back then that I started to worry about her. "Why do you keep hanging out with that Pablo guy?" I asked her. "Are you jealous?" she replied. "No, I just thought that drug dealers didn't make the best boyfriends." "Oh, Pablo's not my boyfriend!" she protested. "Sometimes a girl just needs *it*, OK?"

That ended the discussion.

Years later, I still remember Pablo. This woman is now quite respectable, a steady job, a two-door garage, some offspring and an adoring husband. That poor guy doesn't know about Pablo, and I will never tell him because I know that he just couldn't handle the fact that his beautiful wife, the one who brought so much joy to his life, had once shared her bed with some sketchy drug dealer, a man whom she didn't even care about but only saw because she liked the sex. "Whatever you do, don't ever mention any of my ex-boyfriends, *especially Pablo*," she once whispered to me. "My husband would lose his mind!"

He no doubt would because he loves his wife so much and he doesn't want to tarnish his glowing image of her. So I have never told him, but at the same time, I feel a bit like a liar. Why can't she just be honest with her husband? Why do I have to tiptoe around and protect her husband from his wife's past?

I wish this anecdote was just one scene from one particular marriage, but the reality is that there tends to be a "Pablo" (if not several) in just about every woman's closet. In private, they'll tell you they have no regrets about it. "Everyone has to get out and spread their seed, you know," an acquaintance told me recently. She recounted to me her affair with an older businessman at the World Bank, who took her as a lover when she was still in her teens. "Does your husband know about him?" I asked. "Oh *him*?" she said, as if her soul mate were a complete stranger. "God no! I could never tell *him* about that!"

And there it was again. This woman was willing to tell any random person, including another man, about her sexual exploits, but not her own husband. Better to keep him in the dark than frighten him with the truth, she most likely thought. What he doesn't know won't hurt him!

Except that it will, because one can only keep the truth buried in the cellar for so long before it starts to stink. And so, sooner or later, you and your husband will be drinking coffee at an airport when the Pablo of yore turns around with a grande latte in his hand and says, "Oh, baby, it's you! I haven't seen you in ages!" And then there will be kisses on the cheek and awkward body language, nervous laughter and light sweats and a lot of thinking because when your husband asks, "Who was that guy? Where do you know him from?" after Pablo leaves with his grande latte, you'd better come up with a good, believable answer.

Or you could just tell the truth.

Anyway, it interests me what makes us men so squeamish about these things. Do we still hold dear these pure 19th century romantic images of virtuous womanhood? And how can these old-fashioned ideals do us any good if our own wives can't tell us the truth about their pasts?

The reasons for these ideas stretch deep into the abyss of human psychology. But one reason I have come up with, is that we men are uncomfortable with our own pasts and, especially, with the rotten bastards we used to be. Do I regret who I used to be? Sometimes I do. But I wouldn't ever change it, because it was part of my journey in life.

And so, if I see the proverbial Pablo at the airport café, I won't feel threatened, no, I'll shake his hand, give him a pat on the back, maybe even a kiss on each cheek. I'll take him as a brother, because, I know with great certainty, that woman who's standing there behind him, whom he now calls his beloved wife, has plenty of "Pablos" of her very own.

First Love

She asked to meet at the library, and when we got together she told me her story. One of the more popular boys in our school—a funny musician—had asked her to be his girlfriend. Most of the girls in our school would have liked to go out with this guy. But the new pair had a little problem. "When I kiss him, I feel like I am kissing my brother."

And so she decided to ask me a favor. Would I like to be her new boyfriend? That way, she would have a good excuse to end their relationship.

As you can imagine, I said yes. We walked back from the library to my house. It was cold and our bodies were close. Most of the time, we said nothing. "It's so nice to be with you," she said. "What do you mean?" "It just is."

There was nobody else at home but us. We sat on a couch and watched a TV program called "Fireplace"—it basically showed a fire burning in a fireplace around the clock so that people who didn't have fireplaces could still get that cozy, holiday feeling.

After some time, she turned to me and that's when it happened, my first real kiss. Warm and wet. I got so excited that my whole body started to shake, so she put a finger to my lips and said, "Calm down." Then a new kiss followed and I imitated her techniques. Outside the snow had started to fall, and the sun was peeking through the clouds. It truly was a beautiful day and I felt, for the first time perhaps, that I was really in love.

Unfortunately, kissing was the best thing about that relationship. Everything else was torture. She was happy to kiss me, but there would be no real affection tossed in my direction. She may have been born into an angel's body, but she had the emotional depth of a lumberjack.

"I don't want a partner and I don't want children," she said. "I want to be free, you know. Like a cowboy!"

But I was not discouraged by this cow… girl. Even as a teenager, you see, I enjoyed challenges. So that years later, when I got together with a woman years older than me, who was headstrong, divorced, spoke a different native language, was of a different nationality, and was until recently living at an ashram in India, well, of course I just had to be with her. Some people go sky diving. I fall in love with neurotic women.

But that first girl, she was the Mount Everest of relationship challenges. Some time after our days together, she decided to date a different sort of person, namely a female. So she became a lesbian. And after that, she went back to being straight. Officially, such people are called bisexual. But I think she was just the kind of person who likes to break the rules just to show that they can be broken. She was a nonconformist, like all the rest who would come after her. Since that time, I've gone from cowgirls to animal rights activists to environmentalists. You'd think that each woman in a man's life would be different. But the truth is, quite often, we wind up choosing the same kind of person over and over again.

Fortunately, I am not the only guy I know with a fetish for complicated women. Take my friend Eamon. From the outside, he looks like your average guy, a typical Irishman who likes to drink beer, watch sports, and play darts. But for some reason, he just has to play with fire. Give Eamon a choice between a wholesome sweet neighborhood girl and some edgy, messed up former lesbian and he'll gladly throw his lot in with the latter. I've seen him do it again and again and again and again. These ladies have different names and occupations, but, in essence, they are the same person. And, as you can imagine, when Eamon and I get together to drink, we have a lot to talk about.

"Why do we choose such crazy women for ourselves, eh?" I have been heard to say.

"But I just can't help it, man," he answers in a weary voice. "Those other girls are so boring."

Technology
Triumphs

I got my first mobile phone in the autumn of 2001. I bought it myself at an Orange store on the walking streets of Copenhagen. I was urged to get my own phone by my trendy and overdressed Danish friends who, like most Europeans it seemed, had been using them for years. That way we could coordinate at which night-club we would meet so we could down Tuborg beer and dance the night away to Kylie Minogue and Jennifer Lopez, which seemed to be the only music they played in clubs in Denmark at that time. I had always disdained new technology. Who really wanted to be available all the time, anywhere? But I gave in to their pressure. When in Europe, do as the Europeans.

Unfortunately for my Danish friends, and my social life, I never managed to use the new phone. It sat in an orange-colored box on my bookshelf in my dormitory room. I tried to set up my account a few times, but every time I called the number on the box, some woman picked up and started speaking to me in Danish. Since it was an automated service, she never replied when I tried to tell her that I didn't understand what she was saying. I got so frustrated with that Danish bitch that I returned the phone and got my money back. I told them it didn't work. In a way, I wasn't lying.

I didn't want a mobile phone to begin with. Nobody I had grown up with had ever had one. Pagers were for drug dealers and guys who wanted to feel like they were as cool as drug dealers. It wasn't until my junior year of college when, while sitting with other misanthropic young men outside the dining hall, I noticed that most of the freshmen had mobile phones. Even more horrifying, it turned out that many had already had mobiles while they were in high school! Can you imagine? At age 21, I was already a cranky old man.

Upon the repulsive sight of the alien freshmen, my friends and I vowed that we never would join the sheep and get a mobile phone. We were free spirits who didn't need to be fenced in by newfangled gadgets. But our pact didn't last long. One by one, each friend went down, joining the herd and getting his own mobile. By the last semester of my senior year at my university in Washington, D.C., I was one of the few left who had not yet given in to the temptation of technology, until my father approached me at Christmas with a gray Nokia in his hands.

"Son," he said, "I want you to have this in case of emergencies," emergencies meaning terrorists flying airplanes into strategically important buildings. I could see it unfolding before my very eyes as I took the phone from his hands, first the new attacks, then the exodus out of the city. Maybe I would walk over the bridges to Virginia or fan out toward Maryland. And then I would take out my emergency phone and call home to let them know I was still alive. "Thanks for the phone, Dad," I would say with a tear of gratitude in me eye.

But that never happened. Instead, the phone sat in the top drawer of my desk, buried under piles of never completed homework assignments. I found it useless. I had a normal land line phone in my room and most of my social life seemed to occur spontaneously. "Hey, want to go see a movie? 'OK.' Great, let's go." The phone sat there so long I forgot it even existed.

By this time Eamon was one of my few friends who didn't use a mobile and he was proud of it. "I'll never get one of those annoying things," he would say, proud of how far he had diverged from the mainstream. But somehow he came across a really cheap deal for a mobile, and finally bought into it. "I'm not a sell-out," he convinced himself. "I need it for work."

Eamon was notoriously cheap and his inexpensive calling plan charged him a rate by the minute, but Eamon figured out that he wouldn't be charged for calls if they were under one minute. He therefore became a master of extremely quick phone conversations. He would ring a friend up and say, "I'll meet you at the restaurant in 20 minutes, OK? Bye!" If you were with him when he made these phone calls, you would see him glance at the phone to see how short the conversation had been and hear him exclaim, "That one was only 28 seconds! Awesome!"

One night Eamon rang my room phone to tell me to meet him somewhere on campus in 10 minutes. The only problem was that he didn't know where he would be in 10 minutes. "Why don't you just call me then?" he said as quickly as he could. "Don't you have a mobile phone?" Click.

Did I have a phone? I thought about it for a moment, and then remembered the one my father had given me. I pulled it from the drawer and, after some clumsy attempts, managed to start the strange box up. I put it my pocket, and headed out.

Ten minutes later, I called him. "Where are you?" I asked. "I'm in front of the university hospital," he said. It turned out that I was right across the street, but a bus had just let out and there were people everywhere. "But I don't see you." "Look under the sign." And there, under the sign I saw a dark shadow with an arm held up to one side of its head. Then the shadow waved at me. It was Eamon! "What's up, man?" I said, approaching him. "I'm glad I brought my phone this time." But Eamon was too busy checking to see how long our conversation had been to greet me.

"Fifty-nine seconds!" he cried out and smiled to me. "Now that one was a really close call."

Saved by
a Volcano

I came through a crowd of protestors on a hot day in
Philadelphia, it was the Republican National Conven-
tion, the year was 2000, there were anarchists break-
ing things, and socialists selling newspapers, and college kids chanting. In the melee, I saw her face on a
T-shirt, like some kind of albino seal pup. The slan-
ty eyes. Those fat cheeks. It was her! The man wearing the shirt began to converse with me, we discussed
our love of the singer, her music. He was chubby, in
his thirties, wore glasses, and looked like a mole.

But there was something different, soft about his
demeanor, elusive, as if he was afraid of me. The man
was peculiar in other ways. His shoulders weren't very
wide, he talked with a lisp. He asked me if I wanted
to get a cup of coffee. And then I realized that he was
gay, and I had to tell him no, there would be no coffee. I was renaissance enough to admit I loved the
singer, but that didn't mean that I was playing for the

other team—maybe he wanted to be Björk, you see, but I wanted to be *with* her.

A poster of the singer hung on my dorm room wall, naked, tongue out, covered only in a leaf, like some nymph out of Eden. But I was afraid of her because she was like some kind of vaginal Icelandic volcano that could erupt at any time and bury my soul like Pompeii in hot lava. To hang her on my wall, to see her flesh each day was to me a political statement, a weapon, a way of retaliating against the commercial ideals of feminine beauty around me.

As men we were told to worship *Baywatch*, to drool over Pamela Anderson, buy her posters, hang her on our walls. Maybe our real-life girlfriends bore no resemblance to the curvy models, but we were supposed to be thinking about them secretly, kissing our girlfriends in New York or Washington, D.C., but really thinking that we were on a beach in Hawaii or California locking lips with Pamela Anderson. It was a lie and it disgusted me because Pamela Anderson never did anything for me, never has, this embodiment of these sorts of livestock-like qualities within which Western womanhood has been constrained, a world of faces and torsos and measurements and nail jobs, the ideal of the perfect bone structure and hourglass figure, a regime under which all females will be ranked according to their conformance to the babe ideal, like cattle ranked for milk output, and our role as men in the equation was not to ask any questions and to support the commercial ideal of what a woman should be. It was our duty.

And then along comes Björk, a little wrecking ball who sang of "Big Time Sensuality" and "Emotional Landscapes." She wasn't "perfect", sometimes she was actually quite grotesque, and I couldn't really look at her without thinking that her breath must smell like that fermented whale meat they eat in Iceland, but at least she was genuine, creative, honest—a genuine communicator, an immediate vision of primitive femininity, this kind of womanhood that is buried in the back of each man's and woman's brain. I knew at first sight that the woman liked to have sex, such a wonderful, sugar-glazed feeling for any man, not that she was flaunting her sexuality like Madonna with her stupid conical bra just to prove something, but that she simply liked sex, the way we all like strawberries because they are delicious.

And the problem was that there were far too few of her. There was just one Björk. There were some imitators, but, mostly, she was considered some kind of demented freak. Maybe it was because she was inbred, or her hippie parents smoked too much pot, or she was dropped on the head as a child. And did you see how she attacked that journalist? Or that music video were she sewed pearls into her skin? When a friend saw her singing in *Dancer in the Dark*, he thought she was a mentally handicapped person. "What the hell is this retarded shit?" he grunted. "Turn it off." He wanted to watch a football game on TV. My friend was a sergeant in Pamela Anderson's army, you see. The pint-sized witch from the big island with no trees had no place in mainstream society.

But when I fell ill with depression in college and didn't leave my dorm room for two weeks, the little volcano came to my rescue. The days came and went. It would be dark and then light and then dark again and I would still be in bed. One morning though I happened to open a magazine beside my bed, one that I hadn't looked through before. And she was inside it, dressed up like some kind of surrealistic flower. And I thought, "This is a person who is not afraid of what people think of her." Then I got out of bed, took a shower, and went outside.

Fathers and Daughters

If I could pinpoint for you the moment when I knew that a past relationship was doomed, it might have been one morning in bed.

"I had a weird dream," the girl said. "I was taking a shower and this man came in and…"

"And?"

"We started making love."

I paused to digest what she had told me. "So, you had a sex dream. Nothing weird about that."

"It's not just that it was a sex dream, though" she started to cry. "It's that he was older."

"And?"

"And he looked just like my dad!"

Her Dad? Oh, Jesus. What do you say to that? I said nothing and tried to delete her dream from my memory, though I recall during the breakup yelling something like, "I'm tired of you and your father!" I wish Sigmund Freud had been there that day in the backseat of

Justin Petrone

the car during one of our last fights. He could have offered the two of us some advice, maybe a cigar.

Looking back on that moment, though, I realize that the girl was lucky. Though her father had recently divorced her mother, she at least knew the guy well enough to have a sex dream about him. In my experience, too many women tend to be estranged from their fathers. Some don't know what their fathers look like. Others don't even know their fathers' names. (Another group of women only think they know their fathers' names, but that's another column.)

If I queried the word "father" among the women in my life, I'm pretty certain a few key words would come up: "absent", "remote", "drunk", "cheater", "dead", and "no information available". For many, the very word "dad" brings up conflicted feelings. An innocent question like, "What's your dad like?" can set off unprecedented rage. I have a friend who gave a boyfriend a bloody nose when he brought up her father.

Of course, there are good fathers out there, but for whatever reason, I rarely stood a chance with their daughters. Instead, cupid paired me with a different set of ladies. One girl's dad was a professional athlete who was always away competing somewhere. Another one was given a very clear choice: alcohol or family. He chose alcohol. And, in other cases, even if the father was still physically part of the family, he was emotionally distant.

In Italian-American families, men often hug, sometimes even kiss (on both cheeks, like in the movies). Once I dated a girl of Dutch extraction and I accidentally hugged her father, a man who only managed to say a few words to me during the entire eight-month courtship. "You hugged my *dad*?!" the girl was shocked. "*I* don't even hug my dad."

Needless to say, I haven't attempted to hug my Estonian father-in-law yet. When I rattled off my list of adjectives to my wife, she chose "remote" as the word that best described him. That's not to say he's absent. He's a dependable sort. If you need some car advice, he's your man. Require some home renovation? He'll be there. But one thing is certain, if those two have hugged in recent years, I wasn't there.

So that leaves us with another question. If I wasn't like any of these guys, what did all these women see in me? Did I just have a sign on my forehead that said, *Women with distant fathers inquire below?* Quite possibly. My mother's father died of a sudden heart attack when she was 19, leaving their relationship suspended in time. Grandma's father died when she was 10. My other grandmother's father abandoned her as a toddler. If you look up my family tree, you'll see a long list of fathers who were just gone or not around. And that meant that the sons of these women learned to be the kinds of guys you could always count on to be there for you. I suppose this magnetic dependability made us attractive to any woman who needed some stability in her life.

Now that I am a father of daughters myself, I make a serious effort to be there for them, not only physically, but emotionally. Even though I am not sure what a normal father of women acts like, I am really trying to be one. As a colleague once told me, though, showing up is 90 percent of the job. It is my intention to show up every day. It's taken me time and, I admit, some trips to the therapist to untangle all these complicated threads that weave together fathers and daughters and mothers and sons. But I am trying.

Every Chick
Has a Car Nowadays...

How doth the little crocodile
Improve his shining tail,
And pour the waters of the Nile
On every golden scale!

This is the setting, a parking lot in Tartu, Estonia's second largest city, the home of its oldest university, a place that has educated me time and again in the trade and mystery of the Estonians. But, back to the parking lot...

The parking lot is situated on top of a hill. To the rear stands the university library, across the street is the Vanemuine Theater. Both buildings are culturally significant, both are sprawling masses of gray. Neither has any discernible shape. The day is gray and misty. The parking lot accommodates the maximum number of vehicles.

It also accommodates some local characters. My daughters, two little girls who have eaten too much ice cream, running around the (mostly) dry fountain in front of the library.

Justin Petrone

73

Then there is our friend Kristjan, a wiry Estonian man in his mid-thirties, a globetrotter with an intense loathing of inequality. When he is not backpacking around South America, Kristjan studies economics.

I'm here too, with all of my Roberto-Benigni-meets-Luciano-Pavarotti awkward gestures and jerky body movements, dressed in a gray coat and cap. Like many fathers of small children, I am in need of a shave and haircut.

Finally, there is our main character, a young woman, perhaps in her early twenties, dressed in a white leather fringe jacket and tight jeans. The woman is *tiny*, she stands as tall as my elbows. She has long blonde hair that may or may not be genuine, and one of those thick eyelash jobs that consist of generous helpings of mascara and tiny false pearls.

The young woman approaches me. *Kas te saate mind aidata?* ("Can you help me?") she asks. *Mul on aku tühi. Kas teil krokadiilid on?* ("My battery is empty. Do you have any crocodiles?")

Now, my brain is a bit slower than usual, perhaps because I have just consumed a giant glass of melted ice cream at La Dolce Vita, Tartu's famous Italian restaurant. Still, it processes that she needs my help and that her car battery is empty.

It's the last bit though, about the crocodiles, that throws me off. In the distance, my children are running wild in front of a sculpture of the revered semiotician Juri Lotman's profile. Kristjan is watching them from beneath his adventurer's fedora hat and maybe wishing he was back in Panama or Venezuela.

Krokodiilid? ("Crocodiles?") I ask the woman, just to be sure.

Jah, krokodiilid, ("Yes, crocodiles") she answers me and blinks with those false pearls.

Then I mumble something like, "I'm sorry," to the young woman and walk away toward my car. And as I walk I start to think about crocodiles. I think about their big jaws. A certain poem by Lewis Carroll comes to mind. I think about how if the woman's car battery is empty, someone will have to jump the car. To do that would require jumper cables. Then something clicks in my tired, ice cream-iced-over brain. The jumper cables resemble the jaws of a crocodile! Perhaps the animal-obsessed Estonians refer to jumper cables as *krokodiilid?*

A moment later I am beside the young woman with the cables in hand. I have been saved so many times by other travelers in situations just like this. Now it is my opportunity to return the favor to the universe! The woman shows no sense of relief, and she has no reason to, as my oldest daughter is now tugging at my sleeve. "I need to go pee pee," she says. "I'll be right back," I tell the woman. "Five minutes."

Twenty minutes later, my daughter and I emerge from the library, during which time she locked herself in the bathroom, and I stood outside the woman's toilet, unable to rescue her until an inquisitive librarian inquired as to why the strange man was hanging around the woman's toilet and promptly entered and liberated the frustrated child.

In the parking lot, the woman is still standing in front of her car. My wife Epp has now appeared, following an afternoon meeting with some witches and conjurers at the edge of town. After some light bickering about what took so long, laughter ensues when I explain the toilet situation. Now, to rescue the woman.

I have the cables in hand. I am ready to jump the young woman. But there's one problem. Does red go on the positive or negative? And which to connect first? I look at Kristjan.

"Don't ask me," he says and shrugs. "I usually take buses and trains when I travel."

Now, I am almost 98 percent sure that red goes on positive and black on negative, and positive is connected first. I have done this so many times before. Why can't I remember now? I think about calling my father, but decide against it, so as not to embarrass myself again.

Just then, two men and a woman pass by. I inquire about the cables and they are eager to help. These men speak Estonian. One is dressed in a red jacket. He has the kind of sturdy figure and round face that make him immediately recognizable as a local. His friend is darker and lankier. The woman is dolled up. Long black boots, black dress, blonde (from the bottle), Tim Burton movie makeup job.

While the darker one helps consult the young woman with the broken car on letting the battery charge, the dolled up woman complains loudly to the redheaded Estonian. He answers her back in Russian. Again, I am thrown off completely. Are these guys actually Estonian Russians? Then why did the redhead speak accentless Estonian? Curioser and curioser...

When the young woman's car successfully starts up, I thank the redheaded guy in Russian. *Sbasibo*, I say, awaiting a quick, happy retort in Russian. Instead, the redhead looks confused, as if he doesn't understand the word, or as if I have even insulted him. I then say *Aitäh* instead and he smiles. Then the two men wave to me and rejoin the Estonian Russian woman, who is still pouting beside the car after being neglected for two whole minutes.

Later, on the way out of Tartu, we try to decipher the ethnopolitics of the parking lot situation. Kristjan hypothesizes that the redhead was an Estonian guy with an Estonian Russian girlfriend and that the darker guy was her brother.

"Estonian women prefer to partner with foreign guys like you," Kristjan says. "That means Estonian guys have to partner with Estonian Russian girls. But

Justin Petrone

77

then who do the poor Estonian Russian guys hook up with?"

"I don't know," I answer and shrug. "Uzbeks?"

"Chinese!" Epp proposes from the backseat. She is seated beside our children, who are now fast asleep, their sugar highs finally crashed.

"Man, this country is so confusing," I say to Kristjan. "Estonians, Russians, *crocodiles*. And I would have helped that girl too, if those other guys hadn't stolen the moment from me!"

"Oh, I'm sure you'll get another opportunity to use your, um, crocodiles soon enough," Kristjan says with a grin. "Every chick has a car these days."

One Night
in Bangkok

Whore. It's a word that catches a man's ear. It's the world's oldest profession, they say, and if you have enough money, you can buy a little physical intimacy for yourself, too. Many a great writer has been inspired to write about his experiences in this dark alley of the human experience. And such alleys are especially inspiring when you are walking along them at night with your two-year old daughter.

This happened, believe it or not, a few months ago in Bangkok, the capital of Thailand, when our two-year old daughter wouldn't go to sleep. So I took the little girl in her pink pajamas for a stroll outside our hotel. I hoped that the fresh air would tire her out. But, no, Bangkok at night is even more stimulating than it is during the day: the noises, the colors, lights, heat, humidity. It was all too much. Every direction I turned, I saw Africans and Arabs and Australians and Indians, and everywhere, really everywhere, were the prostitutes!

I had noticed these ladies of the night earlier that day in front of our hotel. I walked out into the morning sunshine to buy some papayas for breakfast, and there they stood, already at work, in their short skirts and plastic high heels. One of them caught me looking at her and gave me the signal: a wink. I nodded back at her because, well, I wasn't sure what to do in that situation. At that time of day, there wasn't one client soliciting a partner from the line of girls. But things were different at night. That's when the boys came out to play, and most of them were old European men. Without shame they accosted the women of their choice, chatted them up, until the two would depart for a nightclub somewhere. I had to wonder— why did they waste their time with the small talk and cocktails? Like the poor girl is going to say no!

"I heard a woman in the hotel elevator," Epp had told me earlier. "She said that she came to Bangkok with her husband, because only stupid women let their husbands go to Bangkok alone."

"I'm happy you came," I said.

"But why do men do it?" she asked me.

"Because they are sheep," I said. "They see one guy doing it, they think, 'If he's doing it, it must be normal.'"

"That's a pretty gross reason," she said and scowled.

Sure it was, but that didn't stop her from going out like a true cultural tourist that evening to see for herself Bangkok's special phenomenon. Not that Bangkok is so special. I've read that there are about 3,000 women in Tallinn who serve foreign men in the same way. As you read this, I am certain several have just turned their tricks and are counting their money. It happens in every city all over the world. But, luckily, Estonian sex tourism is a little more discrete than the Thai variety. You don't have to walk by a line of prostitutes when you take your child out for a late night walk, or go to the café to get some breakfast.

That night in Bangkok, my tiny daughter sat in her stroller, her blonde curls fattened by the late night humidity, her little green eyes taking in the tremendous scene. Some of the ladies even came toward us, pinched her cheeks and said, "Hello!" In these precious moments, they stopped being sex for sale, and resumed being who they truly were beneath the act: average women in a desperate situation. I came to feel like my daughter gave them hope, an innocent snowflake in a blizzard of sin.

Yet all of these women had started out their lives in the same position. If it wasn't for some minor details, my own child could wind up on a street corner just like them. At the same time, they didn't look so unhappy when they got into the hotel's elevators with their older gentlemen dates. Instead, they looked in my daughter's direction and smiled. And the men walked with a certain confidence, as if they weren't

Justin Petrone

81

paying for their dates' company. I watched the pathetic scene and thought about how most of these guys had families at home. Only they hadn't brought their children with them to Bangkok to a work conference, as I, for whatever reason, had done. What kind of parent brings his children to the world capital of prostitution anyway?

But why not, I thought, when I saw that the child had at last fallen asleep. For her, these whores were just pretty ladies. The red light district was just another fun park. And I truly hoped that she would keep her innocence and continue to see things that way for as long as possible.

Poor Mr. Duchovny

One day I went to the recycling center at the edge of town to get rid of some old newspapers. It was late in the afternoon, and the center was closed, but the back door to the center was ajar, so I stepped in and tossed the newspapers onto the mountain of old paper and cardboard. I was just about to leave when I noticed a young woman staring back at me from the floor. "What's this?" I said and kneeled to get a closer look. It was an old *Playboy*. "My lucky day!" I said to myself as I caressed the smooth magazine in my hands, examining it like it was a sparkling diamond. My heartbeat quickened with anticipation.

Then I remembered that I was in public and looked around to see if anyone was watching. All was silent. The coast was clear. I slowly opened the magazine, eager to see the individual advertised as "Estonia's sexiest woman". I was looking for a cheap thrill, something to make me feel more alive, but after flipping through pages of bare-chested nudes, I tossed the magazine back on the floor in disappointment. It wasn't that the women were unattractive. It was just that I was jaded. I had seen it all before.

The first time I saw it, I was about five. I went to my older brother's friend's house one day, only to find a stack of magazines behind the toilet. I remember how I examined one carefully, absorbed by the mysteries of the female body. And I wondered why I had never seen such things before. They weren't exactly lying around on the dinner table. So I knew that what I had seen was special. If it wasn't special, then why would people go through such pains to hide it away?

It figures that I first encountered pornography in a teenager's bathroom. When I was in school, dirty magazines went around like beer or cigarettes. We were too young to buy it ourselves, but someone you knew might have had a connection. Some guys stole it from their fathers, who had vast collections. From there, a kid with good business sense could make a buck reselling the dirty magazines to desperate friends. And so it was passed down, from generation to generation; the secretiveness of the matter only made it more alluring.

This was ages ago, before the dawn of the free wireless Internet connection. I can only imagine that young perverts today trade websites and passwords like kids my age did in the days of magazines and video cassettes. And with the rise of online pornography, it has become a far more open secret. Every day we are bombarded with pornographic links and images in our e-mail. Now you don't need to get your hands on a magazine. It's all just one click away. And a lot of those curious kids who got hooked when they were young haven't given up the habit yet. Now men, they are still addicts, getting their fix on the side, when nobody's looking.

Though no one talks about it, the truth has a tendency to leak out. One of my friends lamented recently that he couldn't access pornographic websites while he was on business in Turkey because such things are banned in Islamic countries. Another, a married father of two, confided to me that he keeps his stash on a special DVD marked *Work for home*. "My wife would never figure that one out," he said. These guys are incredibly nice. It's just that, when no one's around, they indulge themselves.

This is the part of the story where most women tend to cry out "gross!", and it is disgusting. At the same time, they might not understand how sophisticated pornography is. The whole industry is designed to take advantage of men's impulses, to milk them of their money, and pay they do. The masterfully edited images and sounds provoke biological reactions that can become almost addictive. And so-called "porn addicts" do exist. When the actor David Duchovny checked into a rehab clinic for "sex addiction" in 2008, it wasn't because he was cheating on his wife, actress Tea Leoni, it was that his fondness for online porn and sex chat rooms had endangered his marriage.

Some people probably thought him pathetic, but I must admit that I empathized with Duchovny, just like I understand my friends. I know how tempting that world can be when you are away in a lonely hotel room on a business trip and a smiling naked woman is just a click away. But every time I have opened one of those websites, I have felt terrible afterwards, not only because it is impossible to make love to a computer screen, but because I see it for what it is: just another moneymaking scheme designed to prey on peoples' weaknesses.

That Glow

I'm not a hundred percent sure of how pregnant women feel about their bodies, but let's just say that it's not polite to walk up to woman with a big round belly and say, "Oh my God, you're so huge!"

It's just not done, partially out of fear that the woman in question isn't pregnant at all. You know the type, relatively thin in all other places except an abdomen that bulges out from above the waist. "Is she or isn't she?" We've all asked each other about these ambiguous cases. Either you find out from a friend of a friend or you wait a while. If it looks like she's swallowed a basketball, then she's definitely pregnant. If that paunch doesn't get significantly bigger, it probably means that she just needs to lay off the French fries.

But it's unfortunate that pregnant women aren't aware of how attractive they are, because if there is one kind of woman who can magically get my head to turn—apparently without me even thinking about it—it's the pregnant woman, flush with hormones, ripe with life. Of course, all beautiful women catch your eye, but in most cases you can satisfy your curiosity by just glancing at them from time to time. But pregnant women, that's a whole different biological reaction: like some kind of monster-sized magnet, the expecting mother's figure draws my attention. I cannot resist. My eyes have minds of their own.

Partially, I am just happy to know that so many other people are having sex. You'd be surprised. Just today in town I saw a gray-haired woman deep in her forties with a pregnant bulge. Then I ran into a girl with a growing belly at the store who looked no older than 16. My favorites are the very extravagant types: the rail-thin wannabe models who are suddenly found pushing a double carriage down the street in high heels because they've been blessed with a set of twins. I also like the bookish types, the librarians, the scientists; women who at first glance look wholesome, but have obviously done the deed. Biology does not lie!

I used to be ashamed of my attraction to pregnant women when I was a teenager. I couldn't figure out why my head always turned in their direction, but I later became comfortable with it. In fact, I came to embrace it as something from the depths of my subconscious, indeed, our collective subconscious. You've all seen the famous Venus of Willendorf statuette, the ancient fertility icon discovered in Austria, a stone carving of a pear-shaped figure with enormous breasts, a bulging belly, flesh rolling up and down like a hilly landscape. Ancient societies worshipped large women as the embodiment of fertility, the symbols of life itself. And I must admit that I do, too.

Breast-feeding mothers are just as magnetic, in part because their enormous, eye-catching bosoms, but also because some corner of the male brain is simply drawn to those who give sustenance and comfort to children. Without processing any thought, my head will turn by itself toward a breast-feeding mother, my eyes fixing on the milky cleavage, after which the rosy-cheeked woman will tug her shirt up to avoid exposing herself. How embarrassing! But it's not like I even think about it. Something inside compels me to look. I'm sorry!

Not all breast-feeding women pull up their shirts though. There are a few exceptions. We have one friend who will unashamedly reach into her shirt to pull a titty loose to feed her offspring. The first three times she did it in my presence, I tried and failed to avert my gaze as she clutched the shapely breast and popped its cherry-like milk dispenser into her child's hungry mouth. By the fourth time, I became used to the sight of this foreign chest and forgot about it altogether. She might as well have been the Virgin Mary herself, feeding a baby Jesus. This was not pornography, this was anthropology—the big stuff of which life is made.

It's been hard to write this column though, I'll confess. It's hard because my growing family requires my full attention. When one daughter wants mango juice, I get her the mango juice. When the other needs assistance in the toilet, I assist her. But sometimes it happens that my wife needs help straining the potatoes and the older one wants mango juice, the younger one needs assistance in the toilet, and the baby is eating a newspaper in the corner. It's a train wreck. At times like these, I ask myself, "How did I even get into this situation?" Here, I can only blame my biological instincts and hope I can count on them to carry me forward.

"Did You Get Kicked in the Balls?"

That's what a relative said to me at Christmas a few years ago when our second child made its debut. We had traveled across the ocean with five-month old Anna just so that relatives like him could see her. And when he did, he couldn't find it in himself to just say that she was cute. He could only insinuate that by having produced two female children, I must have suffered from some physical problem.

I'm not sure why males are in such demand but it seems that they are favored. When we learned we were having a third child, the prospect of another female made a certain amount of sense. We had boxes of pink clothes packed away. We had the right books, toys, films. And—most of all—we had become relative experts in raising females, at least compared with our knowledge of little boys. Little boys seemed dirty and alien, violent and dangerous. Every little boy I come into contact with is pointing a fake machine gun in my face or trying to saw off my arm. In contrast, little girls seem slightly better mannered…and clean.

And yet, all we heard following the announcement of the coming of our third child was, "Certainly, it's a boy." Sure, it made mathematical sense. There is only a 12.5 percent chance of having three children of one sex. It's not impossible, but it's not likely. But the way they said it made it seem as if we had been yearning for a male child all along. This was not the case. I would have been far more disappointed if I had been stuck with two boys pointing fake machine guns in my face rather than sweet little girls, waking me up with kisses. But to other people it seemed that males were more desirable than females.

Why is this so? It's not like I need help tending to the family farm. I don't know anything about farming. It's not like I need to pass on my talent for building houses, because, as everyone knows, I can't build anything. And then there is the pressure to pass on the family name. Ah, the family name. My grandfather had four sons, so somewhere around the year 1960 the future of the family name seemed secure. But only two of those sons had children, and I was the only male grandchild. And now I am preparing to have my third daughter. So much for passing on the family name! Fortunately, according to the Pagine Bianche, there are 2,208 Petrones living in Italy, so the family name will continue. We have achieved critical mass!

I can understand the male desire to see other males born, if only to rescue them from the wackiness of the female world. There are just some things about girls that I don't understand. I cannot fathom the interpersonal feuds my daughters have, where they can go from being friends to enemies to friends again with the same girl in the same week. I'm tired of sitting in clothing stores pretending to be able to tell the difference between one dress and another. And how many mornings have I rubbed my exhausted face, frustrated because my daughters were unhappy with the way their hair looked? I admit that once in a while, I wish there was another male around to balance out all the estrogen.

But what I find interesting is that some women also prefer boys to girls. When I told my neighbor, a woman in her seventies, that we were expecting another girl, she frowned. "Well, maybe the fourth one will be a boy," she said. *The fourth one?* The third one has yet to arrive and you're already thinking about the fourth? "Boys are easier," the neighbor told me. "Girls are more difficult." Are they really? Hmm, I don't remember many girls playing with pool chemicals or rolling portable toilets down hills, as my friends and I did as youths, when we were out terrorizing the neighborhood.

And how many families do I know where the older sisters are hardworking and successful and the youngest son is lazy and spoiled? A lot. Think about Al Gore. His three daughters have all led successful lives. Karenna is a journalist and attorney, Kristin is a screenwriter, Sarah is an artist. And then there is his son, Al III, who is most famous for being arrested for drug possession, twice.

So, I guess we could try for a fourth, and when another girl is born, we could set our sights on a fifth. How about a sixth? Or a seventh? But, nah. I'm happy with the children I have now, and I have other things to do in life than worry about producing male offspring. Sure, some can joke that I've been kicked in the balls, but at least I haven't been kicked in the head.

The Beginning
and the End

Maria was born on a sunny Thursday afternoon in September. The midwife said she was of average length and weight. Her head was covered in thick dark hair, prompting comparisons to her father, and her eyes were long slits, clearly inherited from her mother. When she opened them she stared around, arching her small neck in different directions, confused by the shapes and sounds that swirled around her.

Soon after, Maria was clothed in yellow pajamas, complete with a small cap tied beneath her tiny chin, and bundled into warm blankets. As she lay there sleeping, with a mysterious and yet knowing smile on her tiny red lips, I took a photo with my digital camera to send to my family back in the US.

Three weeks later I showed the photo to my grandmother Margaret in an assisted living facility. This was after I reintroduced myself to her. Grandma is almost 93 years old, you see, and she doesn't remember who

I am anymore, at least most of the time.

"And you? Who are you?" These were the words she greeted me with as I slid into a chair across from her in a brightly lit kitchen. Just feet away more than a dozen ancient men and women, half of them in wheelchairs, sat murmuring to themselves, their eyes transfixed on a reality TV show beamed from a giant screen suspended on the wall.

"I'm your grandson," I told her. "Justin."

Grandma seemed to recognize the name. "Oh, Justin, that's right," she said slowly. "Well, I sure am surprised to see you."

I would have felt bad to hear those words, as if I had abandoned her by moving to Europe, if I hadn't sat before her at the same table only a week before. But Grandma can't remember that. Sometimes she doesn't know that she is in Assisted Living. She thinks that she is at a restaurant or at home. That's why she is in the dementia ward. According to the ward psychologist, Grandma is convinced it's still 1989.

It is hard to grasp that this is the same woman who was still fairly coherent less than a year ago. She was a little slow, but she could recall the events of yesteryear with startling precision. I asked my father when she started to lose it. "Sometime in the spring," he shrugged. Grandma used to be so proud of her age, too. "I love to tell people I was born in 1918," she would say, "just to see the looks on their faces. Their eyes bulge when they hear it. I get a kick out of that."

"Do you know who was president when you were born?" I asked her from across the table.

"Hmm, let me think," she responded, her veiny hands folded before her. I waited for an answer, but one never came.

"Woodrow Wilson," I said.

"Oh, that's right," she scratched her head, as if she had once heard the name.

Grandma is actually one of the most lucid residents of the dementia ward. The first time I went to see her, another gray-haired woman in a lime green jumpsuit went bananas over seating arrangements, crying, "I sit here, you sit there," over and over again and nodding her head, until I stepped in and pushed her into her seat, saying, "That's right, you sit in this chair right here, and my grandmother sits in that chair over there." "See what I mean!" the crazy lady exclaimed, still bobbing her head. "I sit here, you sit there. I sit here, you sit there." She looked up at me. "He gives us permission!"

The last time I went to visit her, we were joined by another old woman across the table with thick white hair and big brown eyes. "Where do you live?" she whispered to us. "New York," I answered. "Do you have a car?" she asked. "Yeah." "Do you think you could give me a ride home? Are you going to Long Island?" she pressed on further. Then my father interjected, "No, we're not going to Long Island, we're going to Florida today." "Florida?" the old woman snapped her fingers in disappointment. "But I need to go to Long Island," she leaned in again. "Do you think you could give me a ride?"

Just then another younger woman with brown hair approached me, wringing her hands, her eyes swimming in her head. "Mister, mister, can you help me? I just went to the bathroom and…and I did a job in there, but now I don't know where to go," she fretted. "Please help me, mister," she whimpered as if she was about to cry. "I don't know where I am!"

"If I ever get to this point, where I am in one of these places, just shoot me," my father said and shook his head as we drove home. "I'm serious. I'll get the shotgun. I'll write it into my will."

"I feel so bad for her," I told him. "She's in there with all those crazy people. Can you believe that's your mother? She barely recognizes us."

"Justin, she's almost 93 years old," he said, running his fingers through his thinning hair. "It will happen to me, it will happen to you," he sighed. "It will happen to everybody."

To All
the Young Dads

I am a father to three daughters. The eldest, Marta, was born when I was 24 years old. Anna arrived when I was 27. Maria Leena arrived last week. In two months, I will be 32. People enter fatherhood at all different ages. There are teenage fathers, middle-aged fathers, and plenty of old fathers. I'm considered a young father. It feels like I have been a young father for most of my adult life.

I am surprised by how little people talk about fatherhood. All of us, the young ones, the old ones, the in-between ones, are just amateurs, so it seems like we'd all be giving each other advice. But I can't recall any words of wisdom that were passed down to me from my father, grandfather or uncles, except for, "You will never sleep well again." Fatherhood is a lonely institution.

Another young father once griped to me that everything else in life has a manual except for fatherhood. As young fathers, we are content to make it up as we go along, but it would be nice to have a set of guidelines to return to from time to time. I wonder what that list of tips for young fathers would look like. Maybe it would look like something like this:

Time Is on Your Side—If you are a young father, you probably have not yet reached the peak of your life. That means that your salary is dwarfed by those who are older than you, guys with streaks of gray in their hair who drive nicer cars and live in bigger houses. It's easy to develop an inferiority complex in this context, but only if you lose sight of the fact that you are young, and as a young father, your wealth is your health and stamina, energy that can easily guide you through those sleepless nights.

Your Wife Is Not Crazy, She Just Has Hormones—You come home from work to discover your wife has been replaced by some kind of wicked witch whose hair is wild and face is swollen, whose enormous breasts are popping out of her shirt while she clutches a small child in her arms that is crying out in agony. No matter what it is—maybe you forgot to take out the garbage, or stop by the store—this person, who bears some resemblance to the woman you love, is very, very disappointed with you. The things she will say to you will hurt, but you can't let it into your skin. Women who are expecting, and those who have just given birth, are swimming in hormones, chemicals that can make them difficult life partners. To top it off, some suffer from postpartum depression, which can reduce your loved one to a tearful, anxious, irritable mess. All I can say is that you should be patient, hold your tongue, and have faith that there is a light at the end of the tunnel. Despite all those hormones, the person you married will return, eventually.

Reading Is Fundamental—Books for young dads are hit and miss. Some try to appeal too much to a male audience with stupid quips about not having as much time to watch sports on TV. But if you read enough and dig around enough in the literature, you'll find plenty of helpful gems. I learned how to properly hold a baby from reading, making sure to give the kid's heavy head plenty of support, and I learned the best way to change diapers from reading, too. Grab both feet in one hand, lift, and slide the diaper underneath. Simple!

Accept That Your Life Has Changed—When my eldest daughter was a year and a half old, we went on a trip to Amsterdam. Thinking like I did in my backpacking days, I found the cheapest rooms I could fine. But when we got into our room, I was shocked to discover how revolting it was. The carpet was old and smelled, there was a shared bathroom down the hall, which didn't smell good either, and the clientele—other backpackers—didn't look like the kinds of people you wanted your child to be around. We moved out the same day to a nicer place. It dawned on me then, that when you become a parent, you cannot continue to live your life the same way as you did before. The days of sleeping in dirty hostels or hanging out late into the night in pubs are over. In fact, you'll find that your childless friends don't really want to see you that much anymore, because your life has become too "serious" for them. There are two ways to deal with this: continue to pretend as if nothing has changed, or accept that your life has been altered in a radical way. I believe that the second option is less painful.

But Life Also Goes On—The year after Marta was born, I tried to pursue something of a music career in New York. It was something I had always wanted to do. My short-lived music career didn't go anywhere, but I had a lot of fun and at least I tried. Had I not tried, I would have been plagued by feelings of regret about what might have been. It is important to remember that even though life changes with fatherhood, it does not end. Life goes on, both your own and your child's. Parents must continue to seek to achieve their goals, because a personally fulfilled parent is a happy parent who can better respond to his child's needs.

Identify and Follow Role Models—Guitar players try to emulate their favorite musicians, soccer players try to play as well as their favorite athletes. So shouldn't young fathers try to imitate the best fathers? Maybe it's your own father, or it's the guy next door, or even a father you've only read about in books or seen in films. It helps to have an ideal to live up to. Maybe you want to be a strict, conservative father, or maybe a looser, more carefree authority figure. Find the ideal father archetype and study it. If it is actually someone you know, then ask questions. Then try to put your newfound knowledge into practice.

Your Family Needs You—and by family, I mean your wife and children. Your mother, father, brother, sister, grandmother and second cousin's best friend may think they need you too, but the ones who receive the lion's share of your attention must be your immediate, nuclear family. Children are small and fragile, both physically and emotionally. They are depending on you to be there for them to help them when they are in need. The mother of your child bears the hardest burdens in the family. She requires your attention and support. So you have to be there. But don't worry. It's not so hard. As another young father once told me, 90 percent of the job is just showing up.

Let Your Children Lead Their Own Lives—forget about trying to groom your child for success as an Olympic skier or in international business. Maybe she wants to be an accountant or a violin player instead. Rather than trying to mould your child into some image of what you would like them to be, a good father should listen to his children and try to help them reach their own goals. This will make the child's life far less confusing and give them a sense early on that they own their own futures and are responsible for fulfilling their own goals.

Brothers and
Sisters

Two little girls sat in a gravel alleyway in Pärnu throwing rocks at each other. "You stole my babies!" one yelled at the other. "No, you stole my babies!" the other one fired back, pelting her sister with stones.

The "babies" were actually little rocks. For a good twenty minutes they had played peacefully, naming their "babies" who shared a home together on an old brick. "This one's name is Maria!" six-year old Marta held up a tiny blue stone. "This one's name is Villem!" announced three-year old Anna. It was a sunny day, the sky a dream-like blue. What could go wrong? At some point, though, someone took "Baby Maria" or "Baby Villem" over to the wrong side of the pile. And that's when the war began.

I never thought little girls could fight so fiercely. When my daughters start battling though, there are no boundaries. Long-legged Marta naturally brings her feet to her defenses, kicking at her sister's face.

Roly poly Anna reciprocates by using her sturdy strength. Rather than kick from afar like Marta, Anna goes straight for her sister's hair. By the time I wade in to stop a conflict, both are usually crying. "Anna pulled my hair!" Marta will whimper. "Marta kicked me," Anna will whine. I try to console them equally, holding Marta in my left arm, Anna in my right.

"Girls, you should be nice to each other," I adopt my most fatherly tone. "Not every girl gets a sister. It's a special honor." But even as I hug them, Marta will manage to get one of her feet back into Anna's face, and Anna will grab a lock of Marta's hair and pull. "Let go," Marta will growl. "He's my daddy!" "No, no!" Anna yelps back. "He's MY daddy." Anna will tug harder. Marta will kick again. And me? Worn down by the two little beasts, I inevitably collapse on the ground, my two offspring writhing and rolling and kicking and punching and crying all over me.

To me, my daughters' rivalry is a mystery. My kids have the same parents. They live in the same home and so, arguably, are the products of the same environment. You would think that would make them somehow equal: equally parented, equally fed, equally clothed, equally entertained, equally bathed, and, ultimately, equally loved. And yet, they fight over everything: what clothes to wear, what food to eat, what movie to watch: even in a gravel driveway in Pärnu, they managed to fight over rocks.

What is the solution? How do I stop my kids from trying to kill each other? There is some modern idea that if we read enough self-help books, if we go to enough counselors, we can somehow eradicate every problem in existence, including sibling rivalry. There are plenty of self-help books out there, no doubt written by experienced psychologists who have done loads of studies and all of which I am sure would be helpful to read if I didn't have two children to pull apart every day.

I have asked Estonian dads for advice, but their answers haven't been encouraging. "They are fighting all the time," I lamented to Jüri, a father of three young men. "And they will keep on fighting for the rest of their lives," he answered, puffing quietly at his pipe. "They will still be fighting long after you and I are gone." Rein, a father of two grown women, offered a similarly bleak forecast. "Kids," he grunted, "are only good when they sleep."

Real Estate
Roulette

Our friends and relatives call us "gypsies" because we have moved so often. Looking back on the decade we have spent together, I can count 10 different homes. That's one new home for every year!

This might lead some to the idea that I like moving. I don't. It's physically demanding and mentally taxing. And how much of my life have I wasted in home improvement stores searching for just the right screw? Half of my clothes have paint on them. My wife tells me not to complain, that it's normal. Judging by how many other shoppers there are, she's probably right.

This is our shared world, a world of real estate. It's a game of numbers, an inspection of images, of assessing energy bills and sniffing out terrific deals. In Estonia, the agents make sure to include an image of a toilet with all listings, just so you have some idea of what you might be getting yourself into. And then once you have committed to a certain toilet, and the home and land around it, it's time for the renovation projects to begin.

Some men live for renovation projects. It's all they know but I am not one of them. Instead, I write columns in which such men are discussed. See the difference? No. I have no innate urge to build or fix or paint anything, which is why I can't understand why it keeps happening to me over and over again!

Life is short, they say, and I have spent a good chunk of my short life assembling furniture, staining floors, and moving heavy objects. Whenever the day comes when I see my whole life flash before my eyes, it will involve a lot of sanding.

But most of the other men I know spend their time doing the same things. It's normal, as they say.

In these situations, sexual politics rise to the surface. You are less a father and husband than free labor, which would make you a serf of some kind, if you think about it. Sometimes I wonder if women realize what a great deal they get out of being married. We men could be like lions, sitting around in the sun while the women go out and do everything else. Instead we are up at midnight trying to decipher instructions in Finnish so that we can put bed frames together. But it's completely normal, right?

Buyer's remorse. This is what sets in the minute the paint on the last construction project dries. Suddenly, you notice all the flaws with your living area. Maybe it's too dark or the air is too stuffy. Maybe a whole wall is actually rotten beneath the wallpaper, something you probably should have noticed before you bought the place. Maybe the neighbors are smelly drunks. Whatever it is, something will make you unhappy. It's a rule of real estate. It cannot be escaped.

This is when talk of moving resurfaces. Maybe you made the wrong choice, maybe you would be happier somewhere else? For a good amount of the time I spent working in New York City, I had an image of a crooked Northern European farmhouse on my desktop. No matter where we happened to be living, I would stare at that picture and sigh and dream of a life there, how I would relax in some room in the barn and write stories and breathe in the dewy air. Eventually my dream did come true and we acquired such a place, a summer house in Setomaa, but I have never managed to relax or write stories there because I have been too busy with renovation work.

Anyway, as I was saying, it is somewhat unbelievable that after all of that hassle, of finding the place with the perfect toilet and dealing with real estate agents and sitting through boring contract signing sessions at the local notary's office, and then pushing your body and your relationship to the brink by moving and renovating your new nest, you would actually think about finding another home again.

The truth is that sometimes you just have to move, whether you like it or not. This is exactly how we wound up living in Viljandi.

But first, Tartu. We moved to Tartu so that I could attend the university part time, and would have stayed in Tartu. We had friends there, our children had friends there, and it is a cozy town, where we unbelievably lived in the same house for three years. But our lease was up, we couldn't find a new place that we really liked or that would be ready in time. And one daughter's school and the other daughter's preschool were on opposite sides of town. Life in Tartu just didn't seem to be working out for us.

Maybe our standards were too high. We wanted a home where we could walk in a few minutes to a food store, a restaurant, a concert, or the beach. We wanted a home where our children could walk to school. Was that too much to ask? Yet one day, when we had about a month to find a new place, we took a ride west to Viljandi, a town where we discovered that we could do all of those things. If Tartu had wanted to keep us, wouldn't it have made our decision a little bit easier?

When we drove back to Tartu that day, I told my wife, "I have a feeling that Tartu has given us notice that our time in this city is up." Viljandi was reaching out to us with open arms. And so the whole ridiculous cycle of real estate started up again.

Golden Hands

My wife was annoyed with me because I walked past the hammer that was lying on the kitchen counter three times. "I decided that I wouldn't put it away," she said, "because, you know, in most households it is the man who takes care of the tools." With that my face tightened, like a cat about to wretch, and I mocked her in a high voice, *"It's the man who takes care of the tools."*

"Why are you mocking me?" she demanded an answer, "It's true. In most households it is the man who takes care of the tools. It is your hammer, isn't it?" "It is my hammer." "Yes, it is your hammer, so it is your responsibility, as the man of the house, to put it away." "Yes, I am the man of the house."

And with that I dutifully deposited the hammer into the toolbox and was on my way.

I don't think it's the hammer that made her mad though. It's the fact that we have to pay a handyman to paint our rooms and build our shelves. Her father is a builder who knows how to do these things, and she has respect for such men with "golden hands" as they are called in Estonia. Our friend Kerttu also goes on and on about her Latvian father who built the house she grew up in with his "golden hands", and then there is Margit, whose golden-handed grandfather built the house she lives in. Let's not forget Kersti's husband, whose hands are so golden that they "shine when he goes outside in the dark".

And they sort of blush as they praise these golden men and don't understand that Mr. Justin's golden hands write books and columns and articles about complicated shit, and he doesn't have time to paint the office door.

"So, you don't have golden hands," one Estonian woman consoled me. "You have a golden pen."

But it's not the same thing, not in this society at least. Here, physical labor is more revered. Maybe these are agrarian Lutheran ideals that have survived into the 21st century. Or maybe the Estonians still have a bit of that Stalinist Stakhanov "shock worker" mindset lingering in their collective unconsciousness. But when I finish an article, my wife usually does nothing. Creative writing receives more praise, because she's also a writer. But when I do some physical work around the house she leaps into my arms and wraps her thighs around my waist and kisses me with a hot fever like a French teenager rescued from Nazi henchmen by La Résistance, "Oh thank you, thank you, thank you, thank you. You are a good man. You are so kind. Have I told you how much I love you?" Her cheeks grow as rosy as red delicious apples. There are tears in the corners of her eyes. And then more kisses. I have to tug her off of me. "Hey, look, honey, uh, all I did was put a nail in a wall."

Yeah, maybe I am exaggerating, but only just a little. And I am not alone in viewing things this way. "Estonian women prefer Estonian men and it is normal and natural that they should," writes British Estonian columnist Abdul Turay. And for those Estonian women whom fate has dealt a foreign man? "Simple, they Estonianize them," Turay says. "Any guy with an Estonian woman will eventually learn how to chop wood or put up shelves."

This may be shocking, but since I met Epp, I *have* chopped wood and put up shelves. Ikea shelves at least.

Anyway, I think the reason that "golden hands" annoys me is the same reason that it makes the Estonian women around me so proud. In my pop psychology interpretation of things, everything can all be explained by those all-important early childhood years. And when you look at my early childhood years and my wife's early childhood years, very different pictures emerge.

114   When I came into the world, many women in

America were burning their bras. They called it a feminist "revolution" or a "liberation", but whatever it was, young ones like myself were the guinea pigs of the social experiment of the day. Traditional gender roles were reversed. Boys were encouraged to show their feelings, even to have dolls if they wanted them. Yes, it's true, there was a popular children's song called "William Wants a Doll". Want to play with dolls instead of hammers? It was perfectly normal by the standards of the day.

Girls were encouraged to achieve, to be ambitious, to be athletic and tough. Want to be the only girl on the football team? Here's your helmet. See you at practice! And if there were any gender conflicts in children's programming, it was the clever girls who always outsmarted the stupid boys. Always. So now, 30 years later, it comes as a surprise when studies show that many men of my generation in America are regarded as excellent cooks. Women our age in turn have successful careers, many of them making up the managerial class, boasting about what terrible cooks they are.

And we tell ourselves that these things just happen.

Yet one of these wayward, sensitive, gourmet chefs now finds himself in a land where showing one's feelings and making delicious dinners isn't worth so much. There were no bras burned in Tuhalaane, where my wife spent her formative years. There was no "revolution". Boys didn't have dolls. Girls didn't always win. That didn't mean they were all passive. "She is of the rare breed of industrious farmer's daughters," one of my Estonian friends once said of my wife. "Mostly it's these kinds of women who can land themselves a foreign husband." Yes, she is clever, tough, resilient, all of these wonderful things that I was taught to value.

But she also expects that if there is a hammer lying around, any hammer, that I put it away.

This is another country. I have to try to fit in, play by their rules, not vomit every time I hear women gush about some guy's "golden hands". And even if it's my "golden pen" that pays the bills, I must find some time each day to do a little home renovation, just to show that I haven't forgotten what's really important in life—painting doors, chopping wood, and putting up shelves. And if it so happens that I walk by a hammer in the kitchen, any hammer, then I know I must seize it at once and start hammering everything in sight, for as long as I can muster, like a Tuhalaane farmer of old, or Comrade Stakhanov himself, until my hands are so golden with sweat that they shine in the dark.

Fruit Season

I flicked on the light switch and descended the cellar stairs, old and brown and half-rotten planks of wood, each one sloping downward, giving me the feeling that I was falling forward. The cellar is shared by the other family in our house, but until that point I'd had no idea they were using it. The box was heavy, so I had to balance my weight by pushing against the walls with my elbows. They became sticky with dirt and cobwebs along the way. The cellar floor was just dirt and broken bricks. I looked around the small, dim room, and then saw three ancient wooden cabinets, propped up on a corner, the doors held shut by rusty latches.

I stepped forward and opened the first one. Dozens of jars beamed back at me, the light reflecting off their red metal lids and smooth glass exteriors, revealing the contents: plums, apricots, squash. Then I opened the door to the second cupboard. Even more

Justin Petrone

jars stared back at me, proud and modern. Altogether I counted 140 jars in the two cupboards, 37 of which alone contained pickles. Most of them were marked "2012", but there were a few jams that bore the mark "2006". I imagined these were the last resort: what our neighbors would eat in the middle of a thermonuclear winter when they finally ran out of everything else.

The third cabinet was a little creepy. Somebody had scrawled the number 666 in pencil on the door. But I had no place to put our jams, so I breathed in and opened it. It was empty, save for a box of brown, rotten carrots. No gateway to hell here. I tossed the carrots on the floor and slid our two dozen jars of plum juice and jam onto the top shelf, and closed the latch. Then I sprinted back up the old stairs and strode into our kitchen, where I announced: "Honey, the neighbor's wife is even crazier than you are. She's got 140 jars of food down there. She's even got 37 jars of pickles. Thirty-seven! Can you believe it?"

"Normal," my wife shrugged, standing over a simmering pot of boiling plums. "And just think how many she'll put away before winter," she took a spoonful of sweet juice from the surface and licked it. "It's only the start of fruit season." Only the start? For weeks we have been putting away food for the winter. First it was the bags and boxes of strawberries and cherries and blueberries. We even acquired a new deep freezer to store them all in. Next were the buckets of chanterelles. Our kitchen became something of a chanterelle factory. Wash them, slice them, fry them in butter, let them cool and pack them into plastic containers.

When the freezer was at last full, we turned to jams and juices. Last week was apple jam and redcurrant juice. This week it's plums. On one hand, it seems cozy and traditional to make and store food. On the other hand, I feel like I am living with a very strange woman. Of all things a person could do, read a book, listen to music, or go for a swim—she prefers to head to the market, buy a few boxes of fruit, and toil over a hot stove. In my deeply American mind, this makes no sense. Food is always available at the nearest store. If you have a craving for pickles, go get one jar. There's no need for 37! But in my wife's mind, we need to store up. It's as if she starved one winter of her life, and is determined to never repeat the experience again.

It's always been this way. Years ago during our honeymoon, she located a number of yellow mushrooms beneath a tree. Even though we were staying at a hotel and had no access to a kitchen of any kind, she had the urge to gather them, bring them home, and devour them at once. I managed to convince her to leave them there by telling her that they were poisonous, which they probably were but still, I hadn't even noticed them to begin with. This summer we went to Kihnu and rented some bikes to ride around the is-

Justin Petrone

119

land. Near the lighthouse, she started to encounter wild strawberries. A small dot of red on the side of the road would catch her eye and then she would stop and stoop down to gather them. In half an hour, we must have traveled 100 meters, because she had to pause every 30 seconds to collect the tiny forest berries. "I just can't help it," she said to me, a little guilty. "I just have to eat them. It's what I am programmed to do."

Maybe the reason I am more suspicious of nature is because where I grew up on the East Coast of the US, it was hard to tell the difference between the edible and poisonous berries. At least if you got them at the shop, you knew they were unlikely to make you sick or hallucinate. My good friend, whom some regard as a bit eccentric, bought a book on mushrooms just so that he could start to gather the wild ones that grew so abundantly beside the river near his house. Sometimes it was hard to tell which ones were safe to eat. He would leave them under a glass overnight. If spores had accumulated below the mushroom by the next morning, they were poisonous. If they hadn't, the mushrooms were good. He told me that he'd only met one other guy while he was out collecting mushrooms by the river, a Pole. He said the Pole had four plastic buckets, two suspended from each arm. He was pacing around, trying to collect as many as possible.

"Can you believe it? All of these mushrooms out

here and we're the only ones picking them," the Pole told my friend, mushrooms spilling from the tops of his buckets. Then he shook his head and said, "You Americans are all crazy."

Bunny
and Blacky

I like to think of myself as the brake pedal in our family, while my wife and three daughters are the gas. I am as slow as a glacier, while they are speed demons, racing into whatever idea piques their interest. And so, when I started to hear talk of getting new pets, I applied my brake because I didn't want any pets. We have had some bad experiences in recent years. Our last two cats ran away—twice! I expelled another feline from our home because it threw up next to our baby's head. So I decided that I would try and delay the procurement of any animals for as long as possible, with the hope that if I drew the process out long enough, my wife and children would abandon the idea and move on to some other plan.

But, as you know, one brake pedal isn't enough to slow four gas pedals, and Epp is the fastest one. She has a memory of her mother spontaneously getting her a hamster one day about 30 years ago, and she is keen to relive it with her own children. One night, I found myself driving to a house in the countryside to purchase two baby rabbits. One of the rabbits was white, the other black. The girls named them Bunny and Blacky. They cost €5 apiece.

Rabbits! Of all animals! I had been trying to stall the pet-acquisition process by telling our eldest daughter that rabbits were boring, dull animals that were only interested in eating and excreting. The truth was that I had my own pet rabbit as a child. This rabbit's name was Flower. We called her Flower because we couldn't agree if her name should be Lily or Rose or Daisy. For three years, she was mine. I can't say she was the most exciting creature, but she was fluffy and liked to eat straw, and was an all-around pleasant pet. I took care of her as best I could. At one point, my friend wanted to breed her with his guinea pig to create some kind of new hybrid animal, but I said no, though it sounded kind of interesting.

For three years, everything was fine until one spring day when I left Flower outside in the sun and we went to go visit my grandparents. It was early June. The day was cool in the morning but grew hotter in the afternoon, so we placed a call to my older brother, who had stayed home, and told him to go and move Flower into the shade. Unfortunately, he was napping when we called and he went right back to sleep afterward. And when we got home, the rabbit was there in the cage. Dead.

I could only stand to look at her corpse for a second because it was an ugly sight. We buried the little rabbit in the back yard and put a stone over the spot. My mother painted a flower on the stone. It was an experience that I wanted to spare my daughters. Sooner or later little Bunny and Blacky would chew through an electrical cable or choke on a carrot. It was inevitable. And then I would have to watch my children get their hearts crushed and get out the shovel and bury the rabbits in the backyard.

The first few days that Bunny and Blacky were in the house, I did my best to ignore them. I just kept waiting for one or the other to kill itself. Secretly, I didn't want to get attached to them. I have this tendency to try and protect myself from emotional pain, because I know how terrible it feels to lose someone—even an animal—that is precious to you. When I was a boy, long before we acquired Flower the Rabbit, my dog Leroy was my best friend. The mutt was a year older than me, had endured many childlike experiments, such as when I tried to ride him like a horse. Sometimes I tell my girls stories about Leroy, how he was big, black on top, gold underneath, how he would go to nearby restaurants and position himself by the backdoor to eat the scraps, or how we once got lost in a snowstorm together and he helped me find my way back home. I never tell them of how he got cancer and we decided to "put him to sleep" though. I keep that memory for myself.

That's just how it is with animals. Every single one of them I have known has eventually died or will die. Some overheat, others get cancer, others get hit by cars. They come and they go, so why bother bringing another one into your life, just so you can bury it a few years later? I confessed these thoughts to Epp, but she just shrugged and said, "That's life." "I know," I said. "I know that's life."

But what I have learned is that you cannot protect your children from life. They must experience its ups and downs, too. And, mysteriously, Bunny and Blacky have grown on me. These rabbits are quite adventurous. I had to touch them when they escaped from their cage one night. I came into the room and saw tiny dark shapes hopping around my feet. I thought I was hallucinating. When I turned on the light, I saw that the bunnies had freed themselves. So I scooped them up in my arms and returned them to the cage. They continue to break free. I come across these liberated bunnies all the time now in the unlikeliest of places, and I have actually started to like them, if only because they have made my life so much more ridiculous. Imagine, there you are, making yourself a cup of coffee in the early morning, when you notice a white rabbit sitting there on the kitchen floor. Thanks to Bunny and Blacky, our house has become just a little bit more like *Alice in Wonderland*. You can say that I, too, have fallen down the rabbit hole.

Dress Decoded

I arrived in Helsinki with one shirt to my name, a soiled black undershirt that had the misfortune of being the last somewhat clean item in the bottom of my suitcase in Tallinn. I told myself that I would find a new shirt in Helsinki during our overnight trip, something a little more presentable, something simple and cheap. Unfortunately, I forgot that I was in the Finnish capital, where nothing is really simple or cheap. At the Kamppi shopping center, I searched through piles of clothing that looked as if they were designed for anybody but me, loud, striped expensive shirts that would look great on some guy named Kimi or Seppo, but didn't seem to match my simple and cheap aesthetic.

The one I picked out in the end cost me €49, so it was not cheap and it wasn't that simple either, being one of these button-up, collared light blue things with two pockets on the front, one over each breast. The tag said some Finnish name on it, which I had never heard of, making it slightly more tolerable because it didn't say something like HILFIGER across the front, like I'm going to walk around Helsinki and advertise that guy's clothing. And the only reason I wound up buying the thing was because the friendly, attractive Finnish woman at the register saw it in my hands and I, like a reindeer in the headlights, could only nod when she said, "Should I ring you up?" in Finnish.

As soon as I put it on, it didn't seem right. It was tight on my arms, short on my torso (and it was an XL, the same size I wear everywhere else). Moreover, the Finnish shirt seemed like something a rocket scientist would wear (most Finns, male and female alike, have that aloof, academic, rocket science air to them). I mean, it was a fine shirt, and I wore it, but it seemed *made* for Helsinki, *made* for Finns, if you know what I mean, not *made* for New York or Tallinn, and didn't really seem to go with my hairy Mediterranean appearance. So I was walking fusion, the equivalent of mixing Baltic herring with pesto or making reindeer meatballs. Yet, oddly enough, none of the locals seemed to notice the big hairy guy in the weird rocket scientist's shirt. I guess that, to them, I looked completely normal.

And that is the thing about the dress codes of various nationalities, localities, what have you. What is normal in one place, is strange somewhere else. Put a blue shirt on a guy named Räikkönen in Helsinki, and he looks normal, put one on a guy named Petrone in the same place, and he looks like herring pesto.

Like the Estonians, the Finns pass themselves off as some kind of "east–west" neutral zone, a sort of brackish water between Scandinavian order and Slavic bombast. But, just for the sake of pissing you off, dear reader, on that day in the shopping center, I thought the Finns were doing a better job of it. For years I have taken umbrage at the insinuation that Finnish females are lacking in beauty (yes, beauty, one of my favorite topics). But there in Helsinki, I was surrounded by gorgeous women, the kind that firepower 19th century national epics. Why was it so? Finns and Estonians actually don't look so different.

I wandered along in my weird blue shirt, pondering this question. What was it about these Finnish ladies that kept turning my head? Then, it hit me like a hockey puck: *it was their clothes*! It took me a decade to notice it, but most of the attractive Finnish women I saw had a way of straddling that much hyped east–west borderline, so that their shorts were short enough to make you look, but just long enough to not offend anybody. This made them look sexy, but smart as well.

Offended was how I felt a few weeks ago when I returned to Viljandi on a hot day, only to be greeted by throngs of long-legged teenage girls wearing what looked like bikini bottoms. But they were—officially, at least—shorts, and in style, because it seemed like every other 14-year old girl had to prance about Tallinn Street in her underpants just to show off to the uninterested, monosyllabic local construction workers what God had given her.

It bothered me because this is where my daughters are growing up, and, overprotective instincts aside, I wouldn't want them going out looking like that just because I think they would look so ridiculous. Yet here it was all quite normal. When I made a joke about the teenage girls with no pants to a local cab driver, he grunted one syllable and smiled to show that yes, he agreed, it was a little outrageous for a small Estonian town, but that's how it was.

So, I made up my mind. I've got to steer my daughters over to the Folk Music Center, if only because the musicians and artists there dress a bit less, well, flamboyantly. Just remember: sometimes you've just got to honor the local dress codes, if only for the sake of cleanliness. But on most other days, you still have a choice.

Old People
Are Beautiful, Too?

Sure, they are. And I don't just mean aging stars like Sophia Loren or Eve Kivi, *grand dames* who have managed to stay effervescent by the sake of their secret beauty tricks and good genes. Everywhere I go in this world, I see beautiful old people, and, of course, here I mean beautiful older women.

It's taken as a given that men can stay attractive until the day they die. For years, Sean Connery was proclaimed the world's sexiest man. This is a guy who is bald and gray, and yet he's adored by generations of women for his puppy dog eyes and lilting Scottish accent. Age, in Sir Sean's case, does not matter.

But can older women be just as attractive? It doesn't happen every day, but I have had a few run-ins with gray bombshells. Once I was in a mall in Stockholm, where I passed a lounge where people were giving therapeutic massages. I had time to kill, so I decided to get one for fifteen minutes. My masseuse had a friendly demeanor, shoulder-length hair, blue eyes, tan, smooth skin, and wore dark clothes, nothing that would catch your eye. I have no idea how old she was. In fact, I don't want to know. All I remember is the feeling of her hands on my shoulders and back, the relaxed calm that set in when she touched me, and the odd sensation of being attracted to a woman with white hair. She seemed so natural, like biology itself.

Another time I stayed in a hotel in San Francisco, and the owner, a petite French woman, surprised me the same way. She was a curvy lady with an hourglass shape. Breasts like those pomelos they sell at the supermarket. She had red hair, graying at the sides, soft eyes, wrinkled at the corners. I don't think she wore any makeup. And why would she care to? She had probably been married for 30 years! This French woman was very quiet as she led me to the old-fashioned elevator that later bore me to my room. The hotel was plastered with paintings and busts of Joan of Arc, big colorful tapestries hanging from the walls. Some chanteuse was singing on the radio. It was a seductive scene. As I followed her, I thought that for whatever reason, the woman before me was a thousand times sexier than any of the young manicured chicks at the bars in the city's financial district.

But then how come society doesn't see it that way? It always troubles me how, world over, it is youth that are held up as the epitome of beauty and age that is seen as its downfall. People want to be young forever and, as they age, they scurry about, trying to defy time and gravity, dyeing their hair magnificent and totally unbelievable colors, injecting strange substances into their wrinkles to erase them, or to their lips to make them fuller. Some even opt for grotesque surgeries. How about a "face lift" or a "tummy tuck?" Sounds appetizing, no?

But when I think about what I found attractive in the woman in the Stockholm mall or the French hotel owner, it was their acceptance of age, rather than the rejection of it. And there is a hidden subconscious element here too. In some matriarchal Native American societies, it was old women who were respected and adored for their wisdom. Gray hair wasn't something to be ashamed of. It was something that earned you admiration.

Maybe that's what these two older ladies had in common with Sean Connery. You don't see Sir Sean running to the plastic surgeon for Botox injections or a hair transplant. I am sure the man takes care of himself, but he also wears his age with pride and women love him for it. The Swedish masseuse and the French hotel owner did, too. Perhaps that's why I noticed them in the first place.

What Do Women Want
to Read About?

How the heck should I know? Do you want to read about beauty? Fine, I'll tell you my favorite story about beauty. It involves an article I once read in a women's magazine where different women were asked for their beauty secrets and the famous Estonian actress Eve Kivi said, "fresh sperm".

My, how this intrigued me, because Eve Kivi is still so beautiful and mysterious, and I was just up all night thinking about how a woman in her seventies maintains access to a supply of fresh sperm. How could this be? Surely there had to be more than one supplier. Could there be some underground trafficking in sperm-based beauty supplies? Was Sophia Loren in on it too? Catherine Deneuve?

This went on until one day when an acquaintance came by, a young guy, and he told us about how he had attended an event with Ms. Kivi and how they "really hit it off". "Really hit it off, huh?" I said. "Yeah," he answered. "She was really cool." "Really cool, huh?" The bells rang in my mind when I heard this. They rang quite loudly. I didn't have the courage to ask. I could only wonder.

So maybe you don't want to read more about beauty, fine. But what else are they serving up in the magazines these days? New sex tips and positions? This is a topic that always fascinates me because it seems to be a recurring motif in all women's magazines, with eye-catching titles like, "Sizzling Sex Tips that Will Drive Him Wild".

Then there are sex positions. I don't know who is inventing them. Or are they being rediscovered from some ancient Hindi texts? Either way, it is fascinating. How often it is that I encounter articles with titles like "Thirty Things to Do with a Naked Man" or "77 Sex Positions in 77 Days". But it's still just sex. There is no need to make it as complicated as Estonian folk dancing. I've found through the years that the basic positions suffice. The positions in the magazines are mostly just weird party tricks, if you ask me, especially if you have children and you are lucky if you can get any sex at all!

Astrology. That's always fun. I don't think it's completely useless. It helps to simplify life. You can stereotype whole groups of people on the basis of under what sign they were born. Here's my take on the signs: Aries—you're just full of surprises; Taurus—I'm not arguing with you; Gemini—who are you? Make up your mind!; Cancer—it's OK to leave the house once in awhile; Leo—it's not all about you all the time, or... maybe it is; Virgo—you don't have to clean the house every day, you know. You can do it every other day; Libra—this is not a real sign, it's just a placeholder between Virgo and Scorpio; Scorpio—there is no such thing as too much sex; Sagittarius—I thought we were best friends!; Capricorn—you're just a pain in the ass; Aquarius—you're a weirdo and no one is interested in your opinions; Pisces—I love you, but you've got to stop getting yourself into trouble.

Of course, 90 percent of any women's magazine revolves around cosmetics. There are the advertisements, and then there are the stories about average ladies trying the products in the advertisements. Never have I understood this fixation. It's one of those feminine mysteries that only people with two X chromosomes can understand. And yet the little girls in our family are enamored with cosmetics. How many times has one or the other stolen Mommy's makeup kit? The eldest one is coming up to me with dark circles around her eyes and strawberry-red lips and asking me what I think. What do I think? I think you're wasting your time. I think women look their best *au naturel*. That's what I think.

The themes of feature articles in women's magazines are rotated in and out of service. How about—

what do foreign men think of Estonian women? Or what do foreign men living in Estonia with Estonian women think about Estonia? Honestly, I feel as if I am living somewhere near the North Pole. It's freezing outside half the year, everything is covered in snow and icicles, my wife looks like an Eskimo, the language looks like Inuit or Greenlandic, and the cuisine consists of blood and herring. But there's more, articles about self-empowerment and anger management, girls who grow up without fathers, chicks who prefer bad boys, sexual politics in the workplace, and dispelled myths about body fat. You may be who you are, so they say, but with enough fashion advice and tips on hot new sex positions, you can at last become the person you always should have been.

Don't forget the polls. Once I read a worn magazine in the bathroom of a publishing house where women were asked with which Hollywood star they would most like to do it. And all of the little check marks were next to George Clooney's name. If only I could have shown the results to Mr. Clooney! The best poll I ever took in a women's magazine concerned the Spice Girls. Supposedly my choice in Spice Girl reflected my attitudes toward women. Guys who liked Baby Spice were into younger women. Men who liked Posh Spice wanted someone more sophisticated. I chose Sexy Spice. It said that I had a one-track mind!

Every women's magazine is not complete without

columns by edgy writers. Nowhere else can you find such obnoxious tripe, dressed up and made to look as if it offers the general public some deeper insight or valuable perspective. These so-called columnists are charlatans, enemies of the human race. I don't know how they sleep at night.

Mirror, Mirror

It happens at the beginning of each month. I hear the metal close on the mailbox and rush outside and open it up, just to get my hands on that fresh copy of *Anne & Stiil*. It's been sent from Tallinn and addressed to me, sealed in a white envelope. Terrific! I tear open the envelope and hold the soft glossy paper in my hands. What follows has become a ritual. I first flip to my column to see what parts have been edited out of the final product. Then I skim the rest of the magazine, sometimes glancing at headlines, but mostly to just check out the women.

The ladies on the cover are quite attractive, often to an extreme. I found one recent cover so riveting that I had to hide the magazine away under some old newspapers, just so I could go about my daily business of dressing children and tending to the wood-heated furnaces without getting distracted. I won't disclose the name of the woman though, not just to leave you guessing, but because I know that the moment I hold her up as some example of beauty, most of you will start thinking bad things about her.

It's a phenomenon I've noticed with most of my female friends. As soon as I've ever made a remark about the virtues of another female, they've sharpened their spears. "She's an idiot," "she's crazy," "she's so fake," "she's a nasty bitch," and, the absolute worst, *"she thinks that she's so pretty but she's really not."* Ouch. Whatever happened to solidarity? Whatever happened to sisters doing it for themselves? It seems that the competition to be seen as beautiful can be quite fierce. It is as if beauty gives a woman her value, and perhaps it is true. My mother was a slender model in the 1960s. A few years out of high school she was hanging out with celebrities in New York City. I asked her how it was possible. "If you are a young and beautiful woman, you can go anywhere," she said.

But who is beautiful? That is the question. The men's magazines keep serving me these emaciated, rail-thin chicks with fake tans and pointy breasts. After the British Royal Wedding last year I had to endure endless articles about Pippa Middleton, the woman that supposedly all men, including me, wanted. I complained to an English friend about Pippa at a bar one night in Germany. I had drunk a few beers by then. And I said, "I don't see what these guys see in her anyway! She's too skinny." "Well, I think Pippa is quite lovely," the English colleague demurred. "She's your classic beauty, I mean she's nice and thin and trim…"

I should never drink beer in Germany. It only gets me into trouble. And yet I am adamant about my conviction that not every beautiful woman has to be skinny. Maybe I am in the minority when it comes to ideals about body image. Maybe most men and women really do think that the thinner the better. It's lonely to be in the minority. Man, I need to find Sir Mix-a-Lot and buy him a drink.

This all may sound rather silly, superficial, and even chauvinistic, until you consider that my eldest daughter woke up one morning recently and asked me, "Daddy, do you think that I'm fat?" The girl is eight years old. Where does she get such ideas? I can only guess that every beautiful woman that she has ever seen, from Barbie to the majority of the fashion and cosmetics models in *Anne & Stiil*, has been thin. And so she already equates being thin with being beautiful which, as I have already made clear, is not true.

She's not alone. Before she went senile, my 93-year old grandmother used to weigh herself every morning, before and after visiting the toilet. "I weigh 125 pounds," she would beam. She was so proud! But here I was, faced with a little skinny girl who has barely an ounce of fat on her body asking me if she weighs too much. And I was her father. Perhaps I was in a position to rectify the situation, so that she could see the world the same way that I do, so that she wouldn't wind up like my poor grandmother, smiling down at that scale every morning.

So I told my daughter, "You're not fat. You're too thin!" "But so-and-so at school is thinner than I am," she said. "She's also too thin," I said. "You two need to eat more. *Mangia, mangia*!"

My wife told me that maybe this was maybe not the best response, but what is? I still do not know how to proceed. Should I really point out every curvy woman I see to prove to my daughter that one need not be thin to be beautiful? (One time I did accidentally mumble, "nice chick" under my breath as we passed some girls in swimsuits headed toward the beach, and my second daughter became excited, asking me, "Where's the chicken? I want to see the baby chicken!") Or maybe I should take the "You are beautiful, no matter what you look like, it's what's inside" approach. Will that work?

I like to get my wife's perspective on beauty, because we see things in very different ways. Once I suggested that Kate Middleton was pretty, to which she snapped, "Really? You think she's pretty? I don't think she's pretty at all." So, I must have been mistaken that time, as I often am. But recently she caught me flipping through a new copy of *Anne & Stiil* and looking at the ladies.

"Just think, Justin," she said and sighed. "Someday someone will be looking at our daughters the same way."

———————

Gaga Finds
a Way

"Do you want to know what my style is, Daddy?" asked my eldest daughter as we headed toward the stage of the Song Festival Grounds. "Goth."

"Goth?" I was perplexed. Why would this kid want to dye her hair black, wear makeup to make her face look pale, or get her eyebrow pierced? And where did she hear about goths anyway?

"Hey, why do you want to look like you are dead?" I said. "I think you like fine just as you are. Many women pay to have hair that looks like yours, you know. And you are going to dye it black? That doesn't make any sense to me."

"Well, um, I don't think I'll dye my hair black," she seemed to reconsider. "Maybe just wear black clothes."

We were surrounded by legions of black-wearing youth that night, because it was the Lady Gaga concert. I bought three tickets: one for me, one for my daughter, and one for a friend, knowing only that they liked to sing Lady Gaga's songs, a few of which I recognized from the radio, and that they would be so happy to see her. I also thought of it from a historical context. This was something of her generation. A significant event. Years from now she could tell people, "I saw Lady Gaga. I was there."

So, you could say, I was unprepared for what was about to unfold. Not like I was alone. There were plenty of other kids there with their parents. And in the crowd I spied some respectable people too. There was the talented writer Loone Ots. And in the more expensive seats I glimpsed Tallinn Mayor Edgar Savisaar, flanked by two young beautiful women drinking champagne. I can only wonder how Savisaar felt when he watched Gaga arrive in bondage gear on a horse borne by half-nude dancers, or when Gaga danced around with a fake machine gun flanked by plastic dead cows, or when she pulled up her skirt to show the crowd her ass and told them all that she, "Just didn't give a fuck."

"Daddy, she said the 'f' word again!" Marta squealed in delight when she said it. "Why does she use the 'f' word so much?" "Because Lady Gaga is a bad girl," I told her. "Bad girls like Gaga use that word."

How did I like Gaga? The show reminded me a lot of Madonna circa 1991 when she came out with *Erotica* and her book *Sex*, though a bit less raunchy and more accessible for the masses, many of whom were probably not even alive in 1991. But the kids certainly didn't care if she had stolen half her act from the Material Girl. They bopped their heads through "Alejandro", "Poker Face", and "Paparazzi".

"Bad Romance" seemed to draw the most applause, and this is the song my daughter and her friends like to sing together most when they walk home from the Viljandi Waldorf School. I hoped there weren't any parents from the Waldorf School in attendance at the concert. Maybe they would see me and scold me for taking my daughter to see Lady Gaga and not teaching her how to play the zither or recite poetry instead. Or maybe they were there, hiding from me the same way I was hiding from them, feeling guilty for indulging their children in such a guilty pleasure.

It made me wonder, was I a bad parent for bringing my child to such a place? Or would I have been a bad parent if I had not taken my daughter to see Lady Gaga just for the sake of trying not to be a bad parent? What is a bad parent anyway? Being a parent sure is confusing. But I have a feeling that even if I sent my daughter off to a nunnery in rural France, she'd still manage to scrap together a handmade communications device so that she could watch Lady Gaga videos on YouTube. In this way, Lady Gaga is not a yes or no choice. It's more of a choice of how a parent reacts to Lady Gaga than if he or she allows Gaga into a child's life because, no matter what, Gaga will find a way.

I do feel often that I am locked in a struggle between a desire to see my daughter grow up unscathed by the sordid side of life, and a mainstream culture that tells her major focuses should be style, hair color, fingernails, makeup, and pop music. How to find the balance? I don't want to be a rigid father whom she will loathe for the rest of her life, and I don't want her to spend too much time playing Barbie dress-up online.

As a defensive act, I recently signed her up for a co-ed soccer team. I had hoped that by playing a rougher sport with boys, she might shed some of this image-obsessed girlie posturing that she has soaked up from the commercial glitz around her and nurture some other hardworking, goal-focused character traits. Instead, she told me that she doesn't want to play soccer at all and would much prefer to go to dance class.

"Want to see my moves?" she asks with a twirl. It troubles me that she so flatly rejects soccer in favor of learning new dance moves but my wife says not to worry and that I should just embrace her for who she is. "Who knows," she says with a shrug, "maybe she will grow up to be the next Lady Gaga…"

An Earthwork
and a Rhinoceros

There are a lot of good reasons not to have sex with your cousin, but probably the best reason is that you put your potential offspring at a higher risk of inheriting a genetic disease. I know this because I spend a lot of time at genetics conferences. These events are always fun—you get to see old friends and drink wine and eat stuffed mushrooms and listen to talks about the genetics of different forms of cancer.

The liveliest sessions though concern what the geneticists politely call "consanguinity"—the sharing of blood, the state of being inbred. This is actually a big headache for clinicians. They run the child's sample to identify the genetic variant that might be causing the disease, and then they run samples from both parents to see if they also carry the variant. Then, to their surprise, they discover that significant blocks of the child's genome and the parents' genomes are the same. A child born of an incestuous relationship, say between a father and daughter or a brother and sister or a mother and son, may carry 25 percent of the same genome as the parent. This, the geneticists say so politely, is an example of "consanguinity in the first degree".

Watching all these presentations about incest gets me thinking about my Estonian friends. How come so many of them look the same? And, more importantly, how do they know that they aren't related? Especially today, when so many children are born out of wedlock, it is entirely possible that some randy wayfarer could father a child in Pärnu and one in Jõhvi and they would grow up and have a midnight tryst in a parking lot somewhere in Paide and unwittingly have a kid with a genetic disorder.

I ran my suspicion of Estonian inbreeding by my friends Enn and Kaari, but was rebuffed when I insinuated that it was possible that they might be related. They know they are not closely related said Kaari, because they had genetic ancestral testing done. At the time, there were two main tests for ancestry on the market. Men could have their Y chromosome tested: tracing their paternal line back, as well as their mitochondrial DNA tested, tracing their maternal line back. Women, having no Y chromosome, could only trace their maternal line back. According to their test results, Enn's forefathers apparently got to Estonia by way of India, while Kaari's mtDNA was found in the highest percentages in Sami women. So, they weren't related after all. See, Enn is actually Indian and Kaari is actually Sami. Viljandi is a diverse town!

I have always been a little proud that there is little chance that Epp and I are related. Some people are proud of being all one thing, but my kids count among their ancestors Estonians, Italians, Irish, Scots, Russians, English, Germans, Dutch, Greeks and Albanians. Sometimes, when my father drinks his coffee and gets excited, he starts adding others to the list. "You know, my German great-grandfather came from a town on the Czech border," he says. "We could be Czech!" He says it as if I should go out and buy a six-pack of pilsner and place a framed picture of Václav Havel on the shelf.

Needless to say, no one can say what nationality my children most resemble. One of our friends, a world traveler, says that it is impossible to say what they look like. "Your kids are like an earthworm crossed with a rhinoceros," he says. Still, after hearing Enn and Kaari's story, I decided that we should also get tested, if only to have something to talk about in their café. I tested my Y chromosome first, tracing my forefathers back to the beginnings of time. These men were from southern Italy, so I thought that the results would show a migration through Greece or Turkey. Or maybe even Africa! Wouldn't it be terrific, I thought, to discover that I was actually black? Perhaps it would explain my love of African music.

Instead, my forefathers apparently came from northern Italy, southern France, or northern Spain, where the same results are found in the highest percentages. I do have a geneticist friend named Ernesto whose family comes from northern Spain and I have always noticed how we have a similar appearance. At last, I had an explanation! We descended from the same dark-haired, spear-chucking barbarian. Then I ordered Epp's mtDNA test. Her friend, the same world traveler, has seen a photo of Epp's grandmother and insists that she is Jewish. It's in the curly hair, the eyes, and, most of all, the nose, he says. This friend is from the same part of Estonia on the west coast, and tells tale of a caravan of Jewish families who settled long ago north of Pärnu and over time became Estonians.

When asked about it, Epp's grandmother said she had never heard of such a thing, and expressed a general disinterest in our modern genetic adventure, but Epp remained very excited by the idea that she could be Jewish. While waiting for Epp's results, I took long walks near Lake Viljandi and pondered what the discovery of my wife's Jewish ancestry would mean for our family. Would I have to familiarize myself with the Torah? Start eating unleavened breads? Could we still celebrate Christmas? Maybe it would be good for us, I thought, because once Steven Spielberg found out you could count on seeing *My Estonia* the movie in every theater in the world, starring Adrian Brody and Natalie Portman.

But, alas, Epp had the same results as Kaari, a maternal lineage suggesting an origin in Finnic populations and found its highest percentage in the Sami. We were confused. What about the Jewish settlers in Pärnu? But Kaari was very pleased to know that she and Epp both descended from the same little Sami woman." You know, I always knew you were Sami," Kaari said putting an arm around my wife. "You did?" Epp said. "Of course," Kaari nodded. "You look just like one!"

Genetics Wins

I discovered it on the morning of my thirtieth birthday. It was staring back at me in the mirror, sticking out like an icicle or a stalagmite. There, in the sea of dark brown, was a solitary hair, as white as a winter morning.

For a few seconds I deliberated on what to do with the new addition to my left eyebrow. Then I fumbled around for my wife's tweezers, gripped the hair, and tugged it out of its follicle. "That's better," I smiled to myself in the mirror. "As good as 29."

I wished I was still 29. But the truth was that I was 30, and after that I would be 31, and after that, I might be 42 or 54 or 79. The numbers only went up. They didn't go down.

It was a fitting birthday present from my body. The week before I discovered it, I had an encounter with a hairdresser that left my ego smarting. While the hairdresser was cutting away, she alerted me my hair was thinning, a sure sign that all of it would go very, very soon.

"Don't worry," she said, trying to cheer me up. "I'm sure you'll make a very beautiful bald man."

Me? A beautiful bald man? She might as well have kicked me in the balls! I had fallen ill two months before my birthday, endured high fevers for days, and had paid for my suffering with hair loss, a scenario I had experienced when I was in college. Back then people thought I was going to lose it too, but it all grew back, thankfully.

"It will come back, this has happened before," I tried to convince her that it was temporary, but the lady was unmoved.

"Do you have any bald uncles?" she asked.

"Well, one of my mother's brothers is bald," I said. "But the other two—"

"See," the hairdresser cut me off. "It's genetic."

"Genetic? Fuck genetics!" I thought. And the second I got home I began studying up on therapies to prevent baldness. I had chicken for lunch and loaded up on other high-protein foods. Exercise was important too, so I went for a jog. After that, I went to the store and bought up a load of vitamins and hair loss prevention shampoos and sprays. I was prepared to do whatever it took to win the war against biology, no matter the cost.

The seller at the pharmacy gave my full head of hair the onceover as she sold me these items, as if I was the most pathetic customer she'd ever had. She looked very amused, but what did she know? I was just about to turn thirty, and, any day now, I would wake up hairless. The hairdresser had said so. And she was an expert, right? It had to be true.

Or maybe not. When my wife visited the same hairdresser the next week, she was promptly convinced that the mole on her face was an advanced case of skin cancer. Fortunately, a dermatologist diagnosed it as harmless a few nervous days later.

So paranoia was at play, but I have to admit that it wasn't just the hairdresser who was paranoid, it was me. Looks really are important to a person, even if that person happens to be a man. It wasn't always that way. Maybe there was a time a generation or two ago when men never looked in the mirror and didn't mind going bald and getting fat.

In these golden days, the guys just sat around, watching TV, scratching their balls, patting their wives on the ass, content to be married and ugly. But these days the stakes are higher. Just as women are bombarded by images of skinny models that are "forever 21", men have to compete with their male counterparts in advertising.

I was recently asked in an interview to name a man whose appearance I admired. Off the top of my head I said Keanu Reeves, only because when I went to college in Washington, D.C., the black kids on the train used to mistake me for him. "Yo, Keanu!" they would yell out. "What are you doing riding the train? Where's your phone booth?"

Still, a glance around the room of middle-aged male stars reveals scant bald heads, and certainly no white eyebrow hairs. Maybe Keanu Reeves and Johnny Depp and Brad Pitt dye their hair or wear hairpieces, but it really doesn't matter when your wife sees their pictures and then looks back across the table at you.

And if this is a world where a modern woman is entitled to everything, then certainly this modern woman is entitled to a good-looking man with a full head of hair.

This is something I'm loath to accept. To obsess over one's looks though is pure vanity, and vanity is one of the traits that I find the least attractive in people. To me, women have always looked best in the morning before they mask their soft faces with various fraudulent products. They look so natural, so beautiful, so why do they work so hard to hide it all away?

I had to ask myself the same question in the mirror as another white hair grew back in the old one's place a few weeks later. How much damage was I willing to do to myself just to look younger than I was? Tweeze every white hair? Even the dozen or so that were now sprouting on my chin? Spray my scalp with irritants to stimulate growth? No. Nothing could withstand biology, even me. One way or another, genetics would win. So I gave up on the special shampoos and creams. I did try to eat better and exercise though because I realized that, white hair or no hair, you've got to take care of your body. It's really all you've got.

A Big
Difference

Sven and I don't have much in common. He's a builder. I'm a writer. He hates spas and swimming pools. For whatever reason, I find myself in them all the time. Sven is brave; he's a war veteran. I've never been in a war and, as most of my friends would agree, I am a coward. Sven is in his mid-sixties, and I just turned 33.

But there is one thing that connects Sven and me. Our wives are the same age.

The year was 1974. The Soviet Union was stagnating, Nixon was resigning, and most of the men in the world were experimenting with facial hair. Sven was closing in on 30. I was minus five. I'm not sure if my parents knew each other back then. But, anyway, these days Sven is a fixture of my life. I see him at school meetings, children's concerts. We visit each other and make reference to old movies and songs (most of which I know from spending time with my father, who is two years younger than Sven).

It's not so weird for me that one of my friends is older than my father, though. Most of my wives' friends have married men who are older than them, and so much older than me. "A man's age doesn't mean anything," one of them told me. In some ways, that's true. But a woman's age? How many 65-year old women do you know who are married to thirty-something guys? OK, there are some aging film stars and heiresses who have found younger partners, but usually these things don't happen.

The world is full of the reverse situation. Pick up any tabloid, or take another look at your neighbors. It seems that men quite often leave their wives for younger women. That's just how life is. But sometimes this "rule" disturbs my personal life. How often have I heard something along the lines of:

"But Piret's husband knows how to do that. How come you don't?"

To which, I answer, "Go get in a time machine and I'll meet you in 20 years. I'm sure I'll know how to do that stuff by then, too!"

I take long walks by the lake, hands in my pockets. Am I too young for this life? Maybe I should have waited 20 more years before marrying. Somewhere out there I am sure there is a 13-year-old who was just made for me. Of course, our relationship would be illegal now, so we'd have to wait a few more years, but...

Anyway, like it or not, these older guys are a part of my life. I feel like a rookie walking into a locker room full of pros. I see them raise their heads and look in my direction. "And you? What do you know about anything?"

"Just give me time," I want to say. "I'll figure it all out."

But I am not the only one who thinks about such things. Women's magazines are full of stories about couples with big age differences. This, I think, satisfies some perverted longing on the part of the public, so that they can look at the story and say, "What? Those two people are together?" Of course, age doesn't mean anything, these articles conclude. Yet in real life, I think it actually means a lot. At the same time, the theme is beyond polite conversation. It brings out bitter and vulnerable feelings about how things are.

Imagine that two couples meet. One of the couples is about the same age (let's say, they are both 50) and the other is a couple with a big age difference (let's say, a 50-year old man married to a 30-year old woman). Of course, the man in the first couple is attracted to his friend's wife's youthful looks and spirit. And the 50-year old wife is at the same time embittered, because she knows that men can have partners half their age, but women, in general, cannot.

Sometimes I wonder if these older guys feel threatened by me, too. Sure, they know plenty about the world and are maybe better partners when it comes to practical considerations, and even better fathers (because they have the experience of raising children from their first families), but the fact is, they will never be able to get younger. Many of their fathers and mothers are already deceased, or at least very aged. They know what awaits them. In these cases, they might be jealous of my youth.

Still, society seems to favor older men who marry younger women than vice versa. Nobody asked Michael Douglas why he couldn't find a woman his own age when he decided to marry Catherine Zeta-Jones. It would be a ridiculous question. Who wouldn't want to marry her—she's hot! But when Madonna married Guy Ritchie, we all knew that it was doomed to fail. And hasn't time proved society right? Catherine is still standing by Michael's side. And Guy? He divorced his older wife and got himself a younger woman. Normal!

My wife is only five years older than me. But would I hypothetically have a relationship with a woman who was 25 years older than me (the same age difference between Michael and Catherine)? Could you imagine me and Angela Merkel as a couple? But if it did come to pass, you know I'd have to tell everybody, "Love is love. Age is nothing but a number."

And it would probably be the truth. I have heard my older friends' life stories, have heard second hand of the suffering left behind and new joy found. So when my daughter asks me, "Daddy, how come so-and-so's father is so old?" I answer her honestly—how her father was married before but it fell apart and he was lost in the emotional wilderness before he found love again, with someone who happened to be younger than him.

I think it is good to tell these stories in public, too, not just to satisfy the perverse interests of the public, but so that other couples with age differences can feel more confident about their relationships. And, of course, that category includes me.

Five-Thousand-Year
Old Woman

I saw a ghost the other day and I haven't been able to shake it since. It stays with me wherever I go, sleeps beside me, drinks coffee with me in the mornings, and asks me to fix fallen curtain rods.

The encounter happened at a children's museum in Tallinn called Miia Milla Manda. It's a very sweet, gingerbread, Astrid Lindgren kind of retreat. The walls are all yellow and they sell paper dolls there, the pretty ladies who staff it are dressed like apothecary assistants from the first years of the last century. There is a sweet-smelling bakery that serves coffee and hot chocolate, and a garbage can that thanks the children when they throw away candy wrappers and snotty tissues. "Mmm! Garbage! Delicious!" a voice recording says, munching away. "Thank you!"

Inside there is a mock post office from the year 1940, with a quill and an inkwell and filing cabinets for letters. The children can dress up in old-fashioned clothing and sort mail and even send a real letter to one of their friends, if they know the address. One can also listen to a postal worker from long ago tell of his daily routine from a set of headphones on the wall. And above the headphones there is a portrait of Konstantin Päts, Estonia's dictator from the 1930s, which was put up there for the true period effect but is actually confusing because my children think that he is the one that they hear speaking about mailmen's lives 70 years ago.

"See, Daddy, that's the postman who's talking in the headphones." My daughter Marta has told me this both times we have visited, gesturing at the ancient dictator. I look up and there is the deceased *pater patriae* himself with all his presidential regalia, an apparition in black and white. I just nod though when she says it. Who am I to mess with my children's fantasies? The truth will come out someday.

On the wall there is another image, one of three women working in a post office. There are two old ladies in dark dresses with crooked fingers, perhaps from sorting too many fallen apples in fall. But in the middle there is a more familiar woman with hair that hangs in curls and nestles on her shoulders.

That woman. I noticed her the last time, too. The woman is looking down in the old picture, sorting those old letters, but I can make out the lines of her eyebrows, her nose, her cheeks. The woman in the picture is not beautiful in any modern, conventional way but for some reason I feel drawn to her each time I see her, though I can't figure out why.

The last time I was there I stared at the woman for a while, maybe stared at her for too long. And I ogled her so because after looking at that face for so long, I understood at last of whom she reminded me.

My wife's mother.

I shivered when I realized it. It wasn't her, of course. That woman, my mother-in-law, was born a good decade and a half after the old post office photo was taken. But it looked so much like her, and like my wife too, for a very simple reason: because she was an Estonian and they were Estonians.

Estonians. They were a people from a place who had their own capital, their own children's museums and post offices, their own way of speaking to one another, and their own kinds of faces. And I was married to one of them. I was married to an Estonian. We had made more Estonians together. And though I would never know the woman in that photo with the familiar face, I knew her quite well in another and very eternal way.

This was the point where I nearly started to cry and I cannot exactly say why. I almost never cry and I didn't this time either. I'm a guy from New York, so I've been trained to restrain myself from showing emotion in public. But it couldn't stop all of these feelings from

Justin Petrone

163

welling up in me and rumbling and vibrating like some undersea earthquake. That's really the worst, I think. When you feel the moisture in your eyes and you don't even know why it's there.

I think it was because it had been a long time since I had even seen the Estonians as Estonians, as a group of people who came not only with a language and a history, but with a certain set of faces. I had spent so much time in their company that they had only become individuals to me with hard-to-remember names, some odd habits, and a peculiar, often bloody, cuisine.

In fact, if I ever thought about Estonians these days, it was with a mix of disappointment and disgust. Why were those guys always standing around smoking and drinking beer? Why were the women such task masters? Why is there a commemorative book about a Nazi war hero at the supermarket?

There was quiet hatred in there too, nipping at and pestering me. I raked my leaves and shoveled my snow to the best of my ability, just so that I could avoid some dreaded comment or smug look or other expression of Nordic anal retentiveness, because everything had to be nice and neat and within the lines in Estonia. That's how my wife said that things were done around here.

"Damn perfectionist Estonians." I had uttered it hotly under my breath many times. "Snow-shoveling fascists!"

Yet despite the beer and the chores and the Harald Nugiseks coffee table book, the leaf-raking and snow-shoveling and Nordic anal retentiveness, the truth was that I spent most of my nights sleeping beside an Estonian. I had never met this Estonian's mother and never will, because she is dead, but I knew her in some way because she was an Estonian, too. In a way, I had been just as intimate with the ghost of the woman in the picture in the museum.

"What are you looking at, Daddy?"

"What? Huh?" My daughter Marta startled me and when I looked down I saw *her* again. Another Estonian.

"Um, I'm going to go play in the other room, OK?"

"Sure thing, kid."

The eight-year-old skipped away.

How many of them have there been? I wondered. How many women have been born in Estonia who looked just like them? They were all individuals sure, one sorted mail in the 1940s and the other was a librarian in the 1980s and the third was a writer in the 2010s. Maybe one was a bit more neurotic than the other, or another preferred French pop music and a third liked to swim. Yet, in this base, bottom line, at-the-end-of-it-all way, they were all the same person.

There probably had been many more of them. For 5,000 years, they say, the Estonians had occupied this little patch of land by the Baltic Sea. They had come here from the Ural Mountains long ago and handed down not only their looks, but also their language and songs, their knitting patterns and fish-smoking techniques. This, of course, is all well documented, the domain of archaeologists and linguists, most of it kept away in museums.

In *this* museum, though, I began to suspect that they had also handed down something else—their souls. *Her* soul. It was a thought that was both sweet and disturbing. Maybe I wasn't just sleeping beside a 38-year old woman at night. Maybe, in some other, more mystical way, I was sleeping with a 5,000-year old woman, too.

"Daddy, what's her name?" my other daughter Anna asked and tugged at my shirt.

"Whose name?"

"That lady who looks like Mommy. In that picture."

"What difference does it make?" I said and shrugged, and then I saw Anna's little five-year old lips curl into a frown. "Well, maybe her name was Miia," I tried to sound more positive. "Or Milla. It could have been Manda, too!"

"Ah," said Anna. "So this is her museum?"

"Yes, honey. This is her museum."

That's just what life gives you. In one flash you are in the Ural Mountains and the next you are sorting mail and the third you are waiting for your husband and daughters to get back from the children's museum in Tallinn. Life gives you the most important things—your name, your language, your looks—and there is little you can do or change about it. The Estonians were who they had always been, and I couldn't change them nor could they change me.

This thought awakened in my soul a long dormant affection.

Christmas
in Tallinn

I would have walked right past him had two other people not stopped to help him up. And when I saw them stop, I knew they had to be foreigners. Only foreigners would stop to help a disheveled drunk with a bleeding head wound in the frosty streets of Tallinn's Old Town.

"Are you OK? How can we help you?" said one foreigner, a man.

"Your head is bleeding! Do you need help? What happened?" said the second, a woman.

"I have a passport!" the wounded man shouted. He looked to be about 50 years old, and the top of his shirt was unbuttoned. When he leaned forward, I saw the blood stains on the medieval stone wall.

I stood back, ready to assist. The man turned to me. "Can you speak Estonian?"

"Yeah," I said. "Kas ma saaksin Teid aidata?" (Can I help you?) I addressed the drunk in Estonian, but knew it was no good.

"I have a passport!" the man cried and reached towards his inner pocket.

"Oletko suomalainen?" (Are you Finnish?) I tried in my best Finnish accent.

"Yes, I am Finnish," he nodded. "I'm fine, I'm fine, I'm just," he paused to hiccup, "fine."

"Maybe you can call someone?" said the foreign man.

I went into a nearby shop and approached the clerk, a young, dark-haired woman who was texting a friend.

"There's a guy outside your window. His head is bleeding," I told her in Estonian.

"There's a guy outside my window," she murmured, still mesmerized by her mobile.

"Can you help at all? I mean do you have any tissues, paper towels?"

"Paper towels are over there."

"No, I don't want to *buy* them. There is a man getting blood all over your wall outside!"

"Oh, OK." She finally put her phone in her pocket, and pulled on a jacket. "Where is he?" We went outside together with some tissues for the man's bleeding head.

But when she leaned over to give the man some tissues, he threw an arm in her direction.

"I have a passport!" he screamed.

"What am I supposed to do?" she recoiled in panic.

"I don't know. Call the police?" I said.

"The police? I don't know." She looked around and then accosted a round, bearded man in the street and they began to speak in Russian. The man called to someone while the foreigners helped the distressed Finnish drunk up.

"I'll just go back to my hotel," the man said, staggering towards the street. "I have a passport," he lunged towards me.

"So do I," I said. "Are you going to be OK? It's cold. *Kylmä*."

"Yes, yes," he buttoned his top button. "Fine, just fine."

The burly Russian man hung up his phone.

"Is everything going to be OK?" I asked him, this time in English.

"Yeah, he'll be alright," he said and walked away. The clerk also returned to her shop and beloved mobile phone.

"Are you sure you'll be OK?" the foreign woman asked the man.

"Yes, I have a passport, I am going to my hotel," the drunken Finn slurred and limped away towards the Town Hall Square.

On the way up the street the foreigners introduced themselves: two tourists, a husband and wife from Oslo. Oslo! I had been there before. I recalled there were drunks and junkies aplenty lining the streets from Prince Haakon's doorstep straight down to the train station. And yet these two cared enough to help some stranger in a foreign city.

Were the Norwegians just the penultimate specimens of human dignity, or was it just by luck that these two kind ones had passed the drunken Finn, Tallinn's own version of Hans Christian Andersen's iconic "Little Match Girl"?

I bid the Norwegians *God Jul* and felt ashamed for not having stopped by myself to help a fellow human in distress. Had it not been for the Norwegians, I would have stepped over him like a crumpled, day-old copy of *Postimees*.

Was that the spirit of Tallinn in me, or the spirit of New York? I wondered. Or maybe it just was the plain old mean-spirited spirit of indifference.

A Perfect
Christmas

Somewhere in the depths of my memory, there is a perfect Christmas. This is a Christmas that occurred many years ago, when I was a little boy. The anticipation had been building for weeks. My mother had sewn an advent calendar, a felt green wreath adorned with plump little elves and fuzzy reindeer and one very cute and tiny baby Jesus nestled in the manger. Each day we added a character to the wreath. The night before the big day I had gone to sleep, my worn copy of Mauri Kunnas' *Santa Claus and His Elves* in my arms.

Our Christmas tree was modest, not too big, not too small. It stood before the windows overlooking the harbor in the town where we lived, the orange sun rising up behind it. I can still see the stacks of modest toys before me, maybe a bicycle, maybe a record player, maybe a stuffed bear or some toy blocks. I can smell my mother's cooking in the kitchen. Then the guests showed up, grandmothers, aunts, uncles, hordes of children more or less my age. People sat around talking to each other. They ate a hot meal of turkey and cranberry sauce and a dessert of pumpkin pie. Then, after a few more gifts, all wrapped up in colorful paper covered with images of sleighs and snowmen, they went home, and we all cuddled up beside a warm fire in pleasant silence. It was nice.

Our Christmases back home in New York are less ideal these days. When the cousins arrive they typically make straight for the big flat screen TV on the wall to watch the game or spend the evening texting their friends on their iPhones. I don't have much to say to family members since I only see them at these big events, though it is still good to see them. The trees have grown larger in size, the gift giving more lavish, the meals grander. Our girls get so many presents that I can't remember who gave what. When all the guests leave on Christmas in New York, I don't feel cozy, I feel exhausted, glad that the day is over. I have simply lost my spirit of Christmas. I struggle just to remember what it might have been like.

Which makes the fact that we can celebrate Christmas in Estonia this year a very big opportunity. Here, I'm an immigrant, which means that I can start anew, try to recreate that ancient perfect Christmas, the one that still lurks in my mind, try to rekindle my enthusiasm for the season. But it's not easy, because Estonia isn't that different from America anymore. Just today I waded among the tacky plastic decorations on display at the local supermarket while Frank Sinatra sang "Happy Holidays" above. I might as well be in America. And the hypnotic pull of consumerism is even stronger here. Estonians it seems go even more bananas at Christmas time than they do on Saint John's Day. Armies of buyers enticed by the word "sale" descend on shopping centers, eager to snatch up all the junk they can before someone else does.

Now that I have my own children, I also feel pressure to put on a good show for them. The gifts must be different, special, memorable, and yet I always walk away from Christmas regretting that I wasted so much money on things they hardly use. Last year in a pitch of pre-Christmas fever I bought my younger daughter an expensive glockenspiel from a music shop. "Don't you think it's too good for a three-year-old?" I told the grinning seller, who laughed and patted me on the back and said, "Sure, but, just think, she can play it when she grows up, too!" It made perfect sense to me at the time. So I bought that. And I bought them skis, even though it seems that neither of them have any interest in the sport (and haven't shown any since), and I bought and bought and bought, and still the spirit of Christmas eluded me.

Food is another challenge. I enjoy the overload of gingerbread that comes my way at Christmas time, the hot *hõõgvein*, the elves' morning deposits of choc-olate in my children's slippers, but I have not yet ac-cepted the Estonian Christmas kitchen with all of my heart. There is nothing appealing about blood sausage to me, it doesn't really taste so great, it doesn't look so great, and, there's always the minor detail that it is filled with blood, but, I still manage to scarf down one or two during the holiday season. Sauerkraut, fine; po-tatoes, fine. I'll even go light candles at Julius Kuper-janov's grave. Terrific. It doesn't make me nostalgic though, because it's all rather new. Even though I can enjoy an Estonian Christmas, it still doesn't make me an Estonian.

But I am not giving up. I am determined to do Christmas right this year. No matter what it takes. Maybe it's the right balance of gifts and family fun I am searching for. Maybe I can tolerate a gentle help-ing of Frank Sinatra Christmas Carols bought on sale at the local supermarket, without falling for all the plastic crap I have to close my eyes to avoid. Maybe it is possible to control Christmas rather than have it control me.

I think what I am really yearning for when I think of my childhood Christmases is moderation. Just enough gingerbread, just enough decorations, just enough company, just enough gifts…and a tree that's not too big and not too small.

Ski Culture

Skiing was the warm incubator that hatched me, the golden light into which I emerged as a fluffy yellow chick.

My father had adopted the sport and made us all enthusiasts, bought me skis when I could barely stand, if only that my feet would grow into the boots, or that my muscles would develop the reflexes of an athlete, that I would become a natural.

Part of skiing's appeal was that it was a lifestyle, too, a hobby of the rich and famous that had trickled down through the middle class. How many of the rich and famous have died skiing? And how many poor people have died on skis?

That's America. Estonia's different. In America, we ski downhill. We think that cross-country skiing is for sadists and bores who can't stand the excitement of risking a rich man's death. But in Estonia, everybody skis cross-country because there are so few hills to ski down. And in Estonia, everybody skis because it is part of the school curriculum. It's mandatory. Even when there is no snow on the ground, they bus the kids to Otepää and other courses where they ski on manmade snow.

This has generated much chagrining because people hate being forced to do anything. I understand. I grew up on an island, and we were forced to take swimming classes. The most notorious swimmer in our class was Abdul, a Pakistani who for some reason felt it his duty to wear a white speedo. We were often given five minutes to shower, dry off, and report to the next class. Sometimes I would arrive still dripping.

My wife has related to me similar sad tales of a rosy-cheeked adolescent growing up in the countryside who was forced to ski in the mornings and then to spend the rest of the school day in her sweaty clothes. And a generation or more later, they are still doing it. I've been to her school in winter, seen the ski racks outside. It looks like the French Alps!

And so I took it upon myself in this land of mandatory skiing to ski a bit myself, to acculturate, to live as the others do. I acquired the necessary goods at the shopping center in town: skis, boots, poles, hats, thermal vests—you name it. I also got two sets of children's skis so that I could pass on the sport to my children as my father had passed it on to me.

Of course, they hated it. I couldn't get either

daughter to ski for very long and they kept dropping their poles and their boots came free from the bindings, so I would have to redo them and they would come undone again. After 15 minutes of this, their little faces were red and sweaty, one was rolling in the snow crying and cursing at me, the other was standing still and picking her nose with an icy glove finger. The snow was coming down heavy, the wind was blowing it in my eyes. And I knew then that it just wasn't going to happen, not with us, not on that day. Today, two winters later, little has changed. The eldest whines to me whenever she "has" to go skiing at school. She hates it, she says. She tells me that skiing sucks.

This reluctance to ski has disappointed me, I admit. I had fancied myself as the patriarch of a new Estonian skiing family, playing Anatoli Šmigun to my little Kristinas and Katrins. But that's life. Every day we bury another dream.

My own experiences have been a little better. The first time I went out alone it was a beautiful sunny morning, the air crisp, a sort of placid and silent euphoria reflecting off of every tree, every rock, every icicle, even off of my new skis.

With a deep breath I was off, gliding with ease along the frozen shore of Lake Viljandi, like hot butter sliding across a pan. The land sloped downward, I leaned forward, I was again a natural, the man my father had once dreamt I would be, until I reached a small knoll and my skis would go no further.

Here things became more complicated. The path before me went *up*, but I only knew how to ski *down*. After a few minutes standing there, it dawned on me that I would somehow have to ski *up* the hill using my arms and poles to pull me along, sort of like a man in a wheelchair navigating a ramp.

Other skiers buzzed by me all this time, propelled by their own motion, but because I hadn't yet mastered the ice-skating-like side-to-side swagger of the experienced cross-country skiers, I was stuck. It was a Herculean effort to conquer the knoll, only to find a bigger one right after it. And then there was one after that! So this is what cross-country skiing was like? My daughter was right. Cross-country skiing did suck.

The humiliation didn't end there. As I skied on, I found my old downhill tricks, the ones I had learned as a little boy in ski school, were useless. I tried a wedge to slow my speed as I came down a small hill, but because the skis were so thin one slid right over the other, I tripped, and fell on my hip.

And while I was lying there in the snow, with other skiers maneuvering around me, I considered taking a teacher, but only for a very brief moment.

Here, I admit my own prejudices against the Estonians. While I am glad to admit that I know nothing, they are keen to pretend that they actually know everything. I could imagine the look on my teacher's face. In my imagination, he looked just like Andrus Veerpalu.

"You mean you're in your thirties? And you *still* don't know how to cross-country ski?" Veerpalu yelled at me on the course. "I mean, didn't they teach you how to ski in school?"

Barbarians
at the Fridge

It all came out over dinner. I agreed to make something quick, put the penne to boil in one pot, the broccoli and garlic and olive oil to simmer in another. When the meal was ready my children lined up like youths in a 19th century British orphanage. I ladled a serving on to each one's plate. Then the eldest made for the refrigerator.

"What do you need?" I said. "I'll get it for you."

"Ketchup," she answered.

"Ketchup? For what?"

"For the pasta."

"Are you joking?"

"No." And she went to grab the handle on the refrigerator door, so I stepped in front of it.

"No child of mine puts ketchup on her pasta."

"But I want to!" she cried, and then she pushed at me. I held the refrigerator door tight but she had her hands on it and wouldn't let go.

"Who does that anyway? Who puts ketchup on their pasta?" I asked while we struggled.

"Our babysitter does! She does it all the time."

I let out a sigh and the eldest backed away.

"But the babysitter is an Estonian," I said. Both children looked up at me with inquisitive Finno-Ugric eyes. "Estonians are..." I wanted to say "barbarians", but I stopped myself... "Estonians don't know how to cook pasta so they boil it until it turns to glue. They don't know how to eat it, so they cut it up with forks and knives. And they think that ketchup and tomato sauce are the same things because they are both red." I made a sad face and shook my head. "But, look, it's not the Estonians' fault," I said. "They just don't know any better."

"Are you done now?" the eldest one asked.

I nodded.

"Good, so now can we get the ketchup, please?"

"Fine, you can eat your pasta with ketchup," I said. "But not in front of me because I want to be able to eat my meal without throwing up."

Neither child seemed fazed as I left the room to eat alone. A minute later, the eldest called out to me. "Daddy, there's something wrong with this ketchup! It's too spicy." I returned to inspect the scene. "Oh, well, look at that. That's just too bad," I said, holding up the bottle. "This is curry ketchup. Looks like we don't have any real ketchup left." The child had pounded a large circle of the reddish slop onto one side of her plate, I saw. Fortunately, most of the pasta had been spared.

I used to kid my Irish–American friends growing up about putting ketchup on their pasta, but the truth was that the local Italian communities had a civilizing effect on the other ethnic groups, so by that time they were at least putting some kind of bottled sauce on it with a name like "Presto" or "Ragu". I am not even sure when the idea even crossed my mind that one could put ketchup on pasta. Maybe I thought it up one day, the way a child tries to conjure monsters or aliens. Imagine that. Imagine if someone would be so disgusting as to eat pasta with ketchup. Could you imagine?

I first saw it done with my own eyes in Denmark. The young man in the dormitory sat across from me in the communal kitchen. When I saw that he was eating spaghetti I thought him refined. But when he reached for the dreaded red condiment—and then pounded it all over the luscious steaming noodles!— my heart plummeted like a pigeon egg off the Empire State Building. It was an act of desecration, like trying to fix a Mac Book with a chainsaw. It just wasn't done. But at least that barbarian wasn't my own kid!

I learned all these things as a child. I remember my mother teaching me how to twirl the pasta. It would take her hours if not all day to make sauce. Which is why I find the idea of just pounding some preservative-filled crap onto imported pasta to be so shameful.

My internal sense of culinary superiority has gotten me in trouble elsewhere in this land. When asked by a tabloid about what I didn't like about Estonia, I said the obligatory consumption on all holidays of pork byproducts and beer. I was trying to be original! Everybody bitches about the weather. For this I was labeled a "health fascist" and accused of spitting in the eyes of the Estonian people by insulting their cuisine.

Cuisine? I thought. These poor Estonians actually think that their sausages and beer are *cuisine?* But I didn't say anything else. I laid low. I still want to be able to walk down the street and avoid eye contact with my neighbors in peace, like everybody else, you know. And I guess I should be less judgmental. Let the kids have their ketchup. Lead by example. Deeds, not words. This is my lot in life. Had I married a German, I'd be up to my neck in sauerkraut and bratwurst. An English woman and I would be sneezing tea and farting crumpets. A Greek and I would be stomping grapes and slaughtering goats. And it could be worse. They could be eating their pasta with mayonnaise.

Let Her Go

"If you love somebody," once sang British renaissance man Sting, "set them free."

Whenever I hear the words to this song, wherever I happened to be, in a supermarket or home improvement store or hair salon, the kinds of places they play Sting's music, I ponder their meaning.

What was Sting talking about in that song? Should I rouse my wife one morning at 5 am and escort her to the front door in her pajamas—"Here you are, honey, I've set you free"?

Yet last year I pretty much did just that, drove her up to the bus station in Viljandi and kissed her goodbye. Half a day later I received a text message that her plane had landed safely in India. And for the next 14 days, text messages were our main way of communicating. She couldn't have been freer.

Though I dared not tell her, the trip made me nervous, and it made other people nervous. India seemed distant, impenetrable, the kind of place that could make a little Estonian woman disappear.

A few friends and relatives did ask me, "How could you let your wife go to India?" "*Let* her go to India?" I responded. "I *told* her to go to India!"

It was the absolute truth. We were expecting our third child, and I knew that India was a special place for her, and that it would be a while before she could go there again. A trip to India was a necessity. She would need that trip for the sake of her own sanity and of my own sanity, I'll add.

And despite anxiety about the trip, the weeks without her were fun. Each morning I would get up to make coffee and put on the Rolling Stones *really loud* to wake up the kids for school.

That wouldn't fly with most wives (probably not even the wives of the actual Rolling Stones) but my own wife was far away in India, which meant that Daddy could do as he pleased. I cooked and cleaned and did the laundry and escorted the children to and from school and kindergarten. And I came to respect my wife so much more by seeing how much she does each day without complaining.

Sometimes friends stopped by just to witness the curious sight of the stay-at-home father making pancakes. I had the feeling that a few of them felt sorry for me. "This poor guy has to make pancakes while his wife runs wild in India..." "It's a shame he didn't marry a normal woman..."

Hey, what was she doing over there in India anyway? It's hard to say. According to one text message exchange, a monkey stole her bag but she chased the monkey and screamed at it until it let the bag go. She lived in an ashram, I know that, and there was some instruction in something called "reiki". I'm not exactly sure what that is, but it has something to do with getting in touch with your spiritual side. Beyond that I don't really know what went on in India. In a way, I don't want to know.

When two free individuals meet and couple, they over time become so close, so intertwined that it's hard to pry them apart. I remember that suffocating feeling from prior relationships, those hours spent doing nothing together, drowning in the lethargy of partnership. Think of all the time I wasted sitting around. It sapped me of spontaneity. My desire for companionship had become a prison of my own design. That kind of closeness between two people cannot go on indefinitely. At some point, it is necessary to let the other person go to, say, India, and live her own life for a while.

Because I travel for my job, I get to experience this kind of freedom more often, and it is always refreshing, to have your own adventures, to rediscover your own inner flow. It shows you that you are still there, under all the school comings and goings and pancake-making and laundry-folding, there is someone still there who can still develop and enjoy life. Sometimes when you are a husband and a father (or a wife and a mother), you lose track of yourself. Life is a series of chores and obligations. You become numb to the world, which is why it's good to break free, if only to return to the nest, refreshed and with a content spirit.

One of the happiest days I can recall in recent years was lived in Hamburg a few months after Epp's India trip. My work conference was over and I had four or five hours to spend walking around before my train left. I walked that city until my legs and feet hurt, I explored its alleys and churches and bookshops, drank its beers, consumed its delicacies. While I was coming over a bridge, I saw a reflection of my face in a car window. It was the most enormous grin I had mustered on my own in as long as I can remember. I was smiling because I felt free. It reminded me of the look on Epp's face when she had landed in Tallinn after her trip to India.

Workers of the
World Unite

I called my friend on a Saturday afternoon. I figured he was at home, maybe watching TV or playing with his year-old son, but he was on his laptop working.

"What are you doing working on a Saturday afternoon?" I asked him.

"Because I have to, duh," he said, joking but also a little offended. "Not all of us have cushy jobs like you."

Do I really have a cushy job? Before I observed my friend's grueling work schedule during a recent trip home to the US, I thought my job was pretty demanding. Now, I am not so sure. I imagine that some occupations still have set hours, something like 9 am to 5 pm, five days a week, with extra pay for overtime. When you are a journalist with an international beat like me, though, you work long hours so that you can get in those interviews with sources in Tokyo and San Francisco all in one day and type up the news the next.

My wife's work schedule isn't much better. Too many times in the past have I caught her in the kitchen with the light on at four in the morning, editing a manuscript on her laptop at the last moment, or answering work-related mails on her phone while she's supposed to be on vacation.

The availability of technology that allows us to work virtually anywhere at any time is both a blessing and a curse, and I am not the first to observe this. But if the 21st century ideal is to work smart using new technology instead of working hard like we used to, then why does it seem that people are working so much more?

My friend's excuse is that he's in management. He's the vice president of a firm, which means that he oversees a team of other workers, and when one of them doesn't do his job, my friend has to step in at the last minute and take over. This leaves him working on weekends, late at nights. It's common for him to roll in home from the office at midnight and be out the door in the morning at half past seven. He spent most of his recent birthday on a conference call trying to avert another company crisis.

I understand his devotion to his job. If my friend didn't work as hard as he did, then someone else from New York's competitive labor market would step in and take over, pledging to be available to work even more, around the clock, all the time, for less money. That seems to be the way that employment is defined in today's economy. Prodded on by other workaholics, you are expected to be accessible to serve your employers at all times. But, I wonder, if you have to be a worker all the time, then when exactly do you get to be a parent or a spouse? Are you supposed to read your child a bedtime story while refreshing your e-mail every five minutes? Or have a romantic dinner with your spouse with your mobile phone face up, just in case someone "important" calls?

While contemplating this modern work-around-the-clock mentality recently, a strange thought occurred to me. Maybe it's not right that people are expected to be available online all the time, around the clock, to do their employers' bidding. Maybe it's a violation of some fundamental, yet-to-be-proclaimed human right. Maybe we should all go on strike, just like in the old days, turn off our cellphones, unplug our modems, see if we can really work smart instead of getting sucked in to the 24-hour work cycle.

But I don't belong to a union. Do you? Chances are you don't. So there goes that strike option. But something had to give, and recently fate intervened. It started out like anything else. The Internet connection in the house went down and we were so busy that we didn't get it fixed right away. Then the e-mail function on my phone broke, and I couldn't access my work messages using that either. Since I have access in the office, I wasn't that desperate. I just had to plan my days in advance, not get distracted by Facebook and blogs, and try to get as much done within a set period of time as possible, my own personal 9 to 5. And, surprisingly, I found I got as much work done, sometimes even more.

I also noticed right away that I felt more relaxed at home. I really could only read a story to my kids or chat with my spouse over dinner because it was just not possible for me to slip away to check mails. And after a week or two of having no Internet access in our home, we made a decision not to get it fixed. Instead, after years of functioning as an office away from the office, our house became a work-free zone.

I'm thinking about suggesting that my friend consider a similar lifestyle change, to unplug the modem and leave his work at the office, maybe set his own personal 9 to 5. But I don't think he'll do it. He's just got too much work to do.

———

We Thought
You Knew!

When I was younger I would spend the summers working in construction. My boss, Mike, was a family man who loved his wife. But he loved beer more. He slept beside his wife on the second floor of their beautiful home. Late at night, though, his affair with alcohol resumed in the cellar. I know this because one time he sent me down there to retrieve a tool.

"Go get me my saw," he ordered me, and so I was let into his private world of alcoholism. I first noticed the empty beer cans on the stairs, not an uncommon sight in many other basements. Downstairs, though, empties shone from every garbage bin and every corner. "How can he even work if he drinks so much?" I thought to myself. And then I thought, "Does his wife know?"

Apparently not, because years later, after they got divorced, she was livid with her friends and acquaintances. "How is it possible that this went on in my own house, under my nose?" she cried. "And how come nobody told me about it?"

"We thought you knew!" was the response. I wondered if I should have said something after that day in the cellar. Maybe I could have saved their relationship, stopped the proverbial runaway train before it went off the cliff. But of course I didn't. I told myself that it was none of my business.

It's a typical way of thinking. Why bother yourself with other peoples' problems? And maybe I was right. That guy was a full-blown alcoholic. What could I have really done to get him to stop drinking? As far as I know, he's out there somewhere right now with a beer in his hand.

Yet these situations still occur from time to time. Recently, for example, I found out that one of my female friends had a one-night stand. This happened right here in Estonia. It was at one of our publishing house's book launch parties. It was a wild scene. Things got out of hand. And during the big bash, two people snuck off into a back room and...

I have no doubt it was very romantic. The only problem was that the woman in question is married. And I am sure that I wasn't the only person who heard the whispers the following week. Probably everybody who was at that party told somebody else. I didn't know what to do with the information once I knew it. I filed it away with all the other secrets I keep. But, as you can see, I've never been very good at keeping secrets.

So, I decided to share the big secret with my friend Vello Vikerkaar. He's a writer, too, and likes to hear about people and their personal problems. It gives him more material for his controversial columns.

"What do you think, should I tell her husband about it?" I asked Vello. "I see the guy almost every other day."

"Is this husband an Estonian?" Vello mused with the tone of a psychotherapist.

"Yes. But what has that got to do with it?"

"Well, maybe he knows about the affair, and he's OK with it."

"What the hell?"

"You and I are North Americans," he said. "We're more conservative. But some Estonians, they just don't care that much about things like that."

And that was the end of the discussion. Still, that itch was there inside me. Maybe this poor, betrayed man didn't know his wife was cheating on him. Maybe he would soon find out and then I would hear those familiar lines again. "How come nobody told me about it?"

"Because we thought you knew!"

What is a little funny here is that in both situations, nobody kept those secrets. Everybody on our construction team talked about the boss's drinking habit. We used to joke about raiding his beer stash in the cellar.

And I am sure Vello wasn't the only person who heard about the steamy one-night stand at our party in the weeks after it happened. No, those of us who knew what was going on felt fine about sharing such information with whomever we felt like sharing it, even complete strangers. Anybody but the boss's wife or the woman's husband, the two people for whom such information would actually have been valuable.

So I Married
a Writer

At first glance, it all seems quite romantic. One might think of Jane Austen and the stirring melancholia of England in the 19th century. Or perhaps Anaïs Nin springs to mind and with her the Paris of the 1930s, bohemian and erotic. Everyone knows that writers are a little crazy. In my experience, they are, but not in the way you think. Because if there is one thing writers adore more than sleazy affairs, cisterns of alcohol, and mindless self-destruction, it's sitting in one place for a really, really, really long time and writing. Writing is what writers do, and they do it *all the time*.

Here I am reminded of the lamentable suicide of the great Ernest Hemingway, a man famous for fighting in wars and hunting wild animals, but who was plagued to the end of his life by simple hemorrhoids. Think about it. It may not have been the ghosts of the battlefield that drove Hem to the brink, but sitting on his ass all those years, writing!

Justin Petrone

197

And the disease of the pen is contagious. Consider this. While my writer was working on her latest book, I would awaken at strange hours in the night with a feeling that something was not quite right. I'd drift through the darkness of our bedroom to the top of the stairs, from which I would sense the orange glow of electric lighting on the first floor. *Who could have left the lights on?* I'd wonder. Then I would descend the stairs to the dining room. And there she would be, behind the table, punching away at the keyboard, hair in her face. "What time is it, honey?" I would ask. "I don't know," she'd mumble. Then I'd look up at the clock on the kitchen wall. "It's 3 am."

Her latest *idée fixe* is a travel novel, a story of strange men and exotic islands, of scrapping everything in frustration and rebuilding your life piece by piece. When I read the draft, I felt the usual way, like a small boat on top of an enormous tide. From sentence to sentence I felt the water rushing, rushing and rushing, and I kept reading and reading. And the most mysterious thing is that all this water, all these words, all this electricity slipped simply from her fingers in our dining room in the middle of the night.

When I catch her during one of her zombie writing spells, I am grateful that I too am some kind of writer. I lack the near religious devotion to the art that she does, but I imagine that if I didn't comprehend the narcotic-like allure of a creative project, living with such a person would drive me or any other reasonable person mad. And the interesting thing is this: few people write about what living with a writer is like. Everyone wants to read their great books. Who needs to know about the sleepless nights spent laboring behind the keyboard?

There is one more detail. When you live with a writer, you are not only a caretaker who provides energy-sustaining coffees, or a midnight editor who cheers the creator on with her endeavors. Often times you are a character in the books, too. In this world of reality television, there are now reality books, because who doesn't want to read a story that's at least partly true? And so there you find yourself, in fine print, described from another's perspective with lines of insightful dialog that you may or may not recall ever saying.

How does it feel to be a character in a book? You'll know it when it happens. I've come to understand the huge gap that exists between what is written and what is reality. I now understand that even if the scene is constructed perfectly, the dialog edited from a digital recording, it still is not and will never be a precise rendering of what happened. No matter how hard you try, fiction always finds a way in.

I think I am the kind of person who enjoys living with an artist. There are different types of people in this world. Some are analytical academics. Others are fiery activists. But a small group of them are artists; people who can make water rush from their fingertips. It's not easy being married to one of these characters, but it's worth it. After weeks of devotion and labor, she said her manuscript was finished. And it was about time, too! The whole time that she was writing I was jealous inside, secretly jotting my own ideas down in a notebook. I wanted to write, too, but in our family we have to do things one at a time. When one writes, the other looks after the children and the house. This is the rhythm we have found. When one finishes, the other begins.

My Recipe

Marriage is often referred to as being an institution, but to me it is something more mysterious and daring than any bureaucratic, button-pushing office job. There is something cult-like about a life-long partnership with the opposite sex. Sometimes I feel less like I've married her and more like I've joined some new religious order or underground political organization. And the amusing part about this twist of fate known as my personal life is that other people think it's the result of careful planning, executed against a master blueprint. They think I know what I am doing. They think I have the answers!

"I've got a theme for you," said one reader I met at a concert. She was drunk and pogoing in my face. "You should write how a single girl like me can find a life partner!"

Me? I should write it? Why, because I've been married for seven years? I must have done something right, but what is it that I have done? How could I even begin to pass this information along as some kind of recipe that you can try in the safety of your own kitchen? But it's been bugging me ever since. I want to explain, to dissect. I want answers, too. I guess it's only normal.

One thing that immediately comes to mind though, a base ingredient of sorts, is honesty, directness. When I met my partner, she made it clear that she liked me. And if there was any element of womanhood that drove me insane with frustration up until that point, it was the coded manner in which women accomplish things. How many women did I follow down the rabbit hole of mixed messages only to come up empty-handed? But I never doubted that my partner liked me and that made me feel needed, comfortable. So, if you have a partner in mind, let him or her know. Don't waste each other's time.

Thinking back on my previous relationships, it amuses me the extents to which I went to try and impress potential partners. I fell in love with one girl in high school who was a track star, so I joined the track team, naturally, even though I never really enjoyed running, just to impress her. It was madness, idiocy, a ruse: I quit, and I never wound up with that track star, though I was in slightly better shape afterwards. Another woman was a vegetarian. She said it bothered her to kiss me with the knowledge that I might have consumed some poor animal prior to our rendezvous. So I gave up meat. That lasted for six months. When I met Epp, I had abandoned the idea of impressing others. I didn't care how I dressed. I didn't worry about how I behaved. I lacked ulterior motives. In some peculiar way, this probably made me more ready for a serious romantic partnership. So, consider this another ingredient. In order to find a partner, don't look too hard. You don't have to become someone else to meet your lover's standards.

The element that probably most attracted me to my partner was her creativity and her support for mine. In one of our first exchanges, she lent me her Dictaphone so that I could record some song ideas. Later she showed me some drafts of stories she had been working on. To me, this was ideal. In so many relationships, I had pushed my partners to create only to discover they weren't the creative types. They, likewise, weren't interested in my musical or written endeavors. In retrospect, we were just different: and ultimately I have noticed how they paired off with similar partners. The philosophers have found other philosophers. The academics have found other teachers. The attorneys have found love at the firm. And my brother, once a star football player, has found love with another athlete. I would say it's a third ingredient: common interests bind people together.

In discussions with single friends, the question that

is always on their lips when it comes to relationships is "why?" "Why should I invest in a relationship?" "Why should I get married?" "Why should I believe this is 'the one' when a new 'one' seems to come around every few months?" I understand their frustration. People who fall madly and manically in love often look like idiots to outsiders and I must admit that they look like fools to me, too, especially when the fog of passion dissipates. But this is something that has distinguished my marriage from all previous relationships. I never swung from street lamps in the rain, serenading passersby about my newfound affection. I never tried in vain to convince others that I had found "the one". I never thought she was flawless. I knew she wasn't perfect; in fact, it was abundantly clear from the beginning that neither of us were angels. I cared about her though. And after a long time of asking myself why, I instead began to ask myself another question: Why not?

Travels with Dad

One lazy summer afternoon a long, long time ago my father drank 11 liters of beer. He told me this in the Hofbräuhaus in Munich a few months ago while we watched the old men in lederhosen brandish their horns and sing "Ein Prosit".

"And I sat there," he pointed the spot out to me. "Or wait, no, I think it was over here. Yes. That's where I drank."

I was in Germany for a work conference and my father joined me because I invited him and because he hadn't been back to visit in four decades. We've all been hearing about it ever since.

"And nothing has changed!" he exclaimed as we headed back to our hotel. "Even the train station looks the same!"

It is hard to imagine that my father, this man beside me with the gray streaks in his hair, the lines in his face, was once a kid sleeping off a marathon drinking session in the Munich train station. But I have to believe it, if only because of my own tales of drink and debauchery on the continent.

Yet the thing about my father's stories is that they make me jealous. They take place in this magical world of the 1960s, a carefree and innocent time when there were no hard drugs and "all sexually transmitted diseases could be cured with a shot in the butt," as he has told me many times.

"And you know, I assimilated quicker than the other GIs," he confided in me with pride as we drove north to Nuremberg. "As soon as I got my first paycheck, I went out and bought German clothes and a German hat. You would have thought I was local!"

My father's German clothes and willingness to learn a little bit of the language earned him a German girlfriend, though the relationship was over when he called the house one night and her father discovered his daughter was seeing an American.

"That was the end of that," he sighed and rolled his eyes. "And she was so pretty!"

That wasn't the worst thing to happen. A great number of his friends died in Vietnam. "Oh yeah, my sergeant got killed," he said, as if those kinds of things happened all the time. "What about that big black guy you were friends with? The one they called Midget?" I asked him. "Oh, Midget? He got killed, too."

But Dad didn't dwell on these tragedies while we

were in Germany. Instead he was interested in trying out new beers and visiting the Porsche factory or the museum in Nuremberg to learn about the rise and fall of the Third Reich.

At night we went out to restaurants. Our favorite beer was the Radler, a mix of lager and lemonade. It was our first exchange in the morning. "Hey, Dad, how about another Radler?" I would ask. "Want one for breakfast?" "Oh please," he would moan and groan. "I can't drink anymore." But he did. We both did.

One reason for these little intimate moments was the fact that I booked the hotels and forgot to specify that we would need two distinct beds. I had only requested rooms for two people, so we wound up sharing king-sized beds instead. But he didn't mind. "Just as long as I have a place to sleep," he said.

So he kept to his side, I kept to mine, and we slept fine with no complaints, other than when the strippers in the cabaret below our hotel in Munich woke us up at five o'clock in the morning as they called out and whistled to men on the street.

We never set a time to meet in the evenings—somehow he managed to be outside the hotel when I rolled in, or I would catch him at the end of the street. We seemed to be on some other kind of clock, one with a natural rhythm, one that he had passed down to me. We really were father and son.

And yet we were different. Everywhere he went,

women about his age—and younger—seemed to gravitate in his direction, and he would lean in and tell them his stories, and they would blush and adjust their hair and take off their glasses. Then I would say, "Come on, Dad, we've got to get going," and he'd just wink and pretend not to hear me. Then he would continue his monologues about the time his platoon was ambushed by a pack of wild boars in the Black Forest.

"We had to climb on top of the jeeps to escape!"

I learned other things from him during that trip—how older people search for each other in public places, how my father eats until he is full and then not a bite more, how the man can make himself go to sleep. "I'm going to take a nap," he would announce, and a moment later he would be snoozing.

But the more time I spent with him, the more I began to understand that his grand stories of his glorious past were not so innocent and carefree because it was a more innocent and carefree time, but because my father, the man, was still innocent and carefree in his heart.

Can you believe it took me 33 years to figure that out? I've known my father my whole life, lived half that time in the same house with him, but in just a week's time on the road, I was able to learn more about him than I had ever known before!

This reminds me of how Epp and I traveled around Europe a decade ago, after we had just met. Our journey lasted 40 days. During those days, I learned to love her passionately and hate her passionately, but at the end of the trip, I was sure that I couldn't really live without her. I wonder if our relationship would have progressed at such a tempo if we had only met from time to time in cafés and bars.

Traveling is something that can open a window to a person's soul. So now I have a plan to go on a trip with my mother, and, sooner or later, with my daughters, too. Of course, I should also hit the road again with my father. Maybe those big family trips are over-rated. But I now believe that traveling *tête-à-tête* can do wonders for any two people's relationship.

Tip-top Blood

As the taxi bore us out to Mähe, my father asked about a strip of land in the distance that appeared to be disconnected from the mainland. "What is that, is that an island?" he asked.

"Maybe," I answered. Then I asked the taxi driver in Estonian if it was an island, perhaps the fabled Prangli Island, center of an excellent short story by the reclusive writer Vello Vikerkaar. That story, "The Inbred Bastards of Prangli Island", hinted at the lack of genetic diversity on Prangli, which prompted the following question.

"You're not from Prangli, right?"

"No," the driver answered, looking in the rearview mirror.

"Good. So, is it true that all the people who live there are relatives?"

"Well, yeah," he said. "You are stuck on an island, you want to keep the property in the family, so you wind up marrying your cousin. I mean, who else are you going to fuck?"

"You could go to Helsinki," I suggested. "Just row up to the port in the middle of the night, seduce some women, and head back to Prangli."

The driver laughed. "But, you know, we Estonians on the mainland are not inbred. We've been invaded so many times! Germans, Russians, Danes, Swedes, Poles..." he counted them out on his fingers so as not to forget, "...our blood is *tip top*!"

At this point I chuckled, not because Estonians are so proud that they carry the genes of a motley crew of rapists in their blood, but because they overuse the terms "tip top" and "superluks" in everyday speech. Both are English borrowings ("superluks" = "super luxury"), and both are used to describe material things: a new car might be tip top, a swanky apartment could be superluks, but this was the first time I have ever heard a person refer to his *blood* as being tip top.

Estonian genetic diversity was one of the selling points of the Estonian Genome Project, which billed the small country's genetic heritage as being as heterogeneous as, and representative of, the larger European population, just as the older Icelandic project was sold on that small country's homogeneous population and tip-top genealogical records, making it possible to trace rare diseases over many generations and, ultimately, identify the variants causing those diseases.

But that's marketing. I honestly have no idea what real genetic impact Estonia's assorted invaders had on the local population.

I have wondered from time to time what the poor Estonian geneticists will do if one of my offspring shows up in the biobank and they start picking up variants associated with Mediterranean populations, leading to some backward hypothesis—*Maybe there was a Greek in the Teutonic Order?*—when, all along, it was just little old me and my wanderlust.

Or maybe it will be cause for celebration, a vindication of the big theory that the Estonians are genetically diverse, that there is no risk in breeding with your neighbor, so long as he or she is not from Prangli Island. I can just see the beaming geneticist's face as she holds up a vial marked with my surname, the flash in her eyes as she yells out to her colleagues to share the good news. "Our blood really is tip top," she cries out in the lab, "superluks!"

Mother and Father
in Estonia

I think it is good that I married an Estonian person because it saved my family the trouble of me being married to another American person. And there would have been plenty of reasons for trouble, believe me, reasons of religion, reasons of class, reasons of ethnic background. And don't start thinking that a person of your own kind could be ideal, because having two Italian-American "Mamas" spar over who gets to see the grandkids would be painful, not ideal.

By marrying an Estonian, I pushed my parents into such uncomfortable terrain that they struggled for years to come to, to get their bearings, to try and understand how it had even happened that this land, Estonia, had somehow wound up being so important to them, without them really having known where it was located before.

The petty rivalries that afflict my American friends who have married other Americans of different faiths or classes or even those who are the same as them are absent here. Instead, my parents' approach to Estonia is more like that of idealistic astronauts who have found themselves captured and taken to some distant planet by a human-like species that is much like their own and yet different.

The wonders of this strange new planet have astounded them since they first set foot on it almost 10 years ago. Every moment has bred questions, questions I have struggled to answer. "Why does milk come in plastic bags?" "Why is the toilet in a separate room from the bathtub?" "How come so many people hang their clothes out to dry?"

Most of the time, the only thing I can tell them is, "I don't know."

In some cases this has been an educational lesson for me, a glimpse into previously unknown family history, because my parents used to hang their clothing out to dry before the discovery of dryers, too. "I used to hate it so much," my mother told me. "My pants would freeze in the winter. It would be like wearing cardboard." And discussions over wood heating brought up the fact that long ago, before the switch to oil, most people heated their homes with coal. "Oh yeah, we used to have a big coal-burning furnace in the basement..."

My mother has ventured into local social life more deeply, befriending many of our Estonian relatives, especially the younger female cousins. Here, I have witnessed nothing less than a spectacular clash of American and Estonian values.

My mother, like all of us, is a walking time capsule. Having watched the women of her parents' generation struggle with early marriages that later failed, too many children, financial reliance on their spouses, and many unfulfilled dreams, she and many other women of her generation decided some time about 40 years ago that the ideal life was to marry later in life, to delay motherhood until absolutely necessary, to have a career to create financial independence, and to fulfill as many of those dreams as possible.

Imagine then how horrible it is for my mother to encounter 25-year old women with two children who mostly count on their spouses to support them, and whose only goals in life are to be a good mother, wife, and maybe a good cook? For her, it's like a nightmare time machine to the past where women were medicating themselves with prescription drugs and alcohol to forget about the prison of their constricting social role. She thought she would never witness it again, but there it is in Estonia, staring her in the face. And the worst thing is some of these Estonian women seem completely content!

So Mother has become an American missionary. Don't get married young, go out and have your fun! Don't have children at 25, have a career! Many young

Estonian women already live such a life, and don't need the extra lecturing, but there are some for whom it is the first time they have received such messages. It surprises them to hear it. "What? Me? College? A career? But I'm a woman..."

My father is probably the reason I wound up marrying an Estonian in the first place. He is the one who recounted his adventures in Europe to me as a child, making it seem like a magical place filled with beautiful women, full of wonders and possibilities, the real place to fulfill your dreams. And the truth is that Europe still feels that way, at least to me, at least to him.

At the same time, he is a creature of habit. My father wants to have access to Starbucks coffee at all times. It is a must. And since there are Starbucks in most other European nations, he has never been inconvenienced by his sojourns in Germany and the Netherlands. There are Starbucks even in Helsinki! But, unfortunately, there are none in Estonia, not in Tallinn, definitely not in Viljandi. The only place he could get his morning coffee was at the Green House Café and he did, but this lack of access to his favorite coffee has been cause for escapist fantasies like, "Hey, maybe I should open a Starbucks in Tallinn. I could make *a lot* of money!"

Other than the absence of Starbucks, the only thing that bothers him about Estonia is the abruptness of conversation, the hesitance some have about talking. Dad comes from a culture where people are smiling and shaking hands and hugging, even strangers, and so when he asks an Estonian guy a question and gets a one-word response, he thinks he has offended him. "Is it something I said? Something I did?" I tell him not to worry. Some Estonians are just like that.

I have to say that both of my parents are more adventurous than the average American. Most Americans don't have passports, few ever leave the country, some never venture outside of their own state. It's like those petty rivalries I was talking about before. Sure, my marrying an Estonian hasn't been easy on my parents, but for an American from New York, marrying someone from *New Jersey* might cause all kinds of trouble. In that way, such learning experiences come with any marriage between any two people from anywhere in the world.

Virgin Sauna

Big floppy breasts hanging in your face. The flicker of the light of the fire and the chill of lake water on your body and the suspicion a snail might be hanging off your dick. But you just don't care because the heat has sapped all your ability to think critically. At this point, you don't think at all, only breathe. You might as well be a snail or a tree. And trees are all you smell; the sweet aroma of hot wood and hot leaves and then the pain of the steam on your ears, eyelids, lungs, and fingernails. The undulating blasts of the hot air come on strong. Pain, pleasure, curiosity, birch water. These are all things that remind me of the sauna.

In Estonia, the sauna is a cultural institution that teeters on the tightrope of logic and insanity. In winter, saunas make perfect sense. Like some sort of primitive math, the coldest of cold exteriors plus the hottest of hot interiors equals something resembling normal body temperature. In summer, though, saunas make no sense at all. No normal person would even consider a sauna in the summertime. He or she would just go to the beach. Try selling sauna equipment in Rio de Janeiro, see how successful you are. If it's already hot outside, why get even hotter?

So if summertime saunas make no sense, then why do the supposedly rational Estonians relish them so?

I posed this question to my friend Jüri, but he couldn't come up with a reasonable answer, even though he's a highly-regarded professor. His eyes bulged when I asked him one June evening, "Why do Estonians take saunas in the summertime?"

In response, total silence. Jüri was truly perplexed. He stared at his feet like he usually does when asked for his wisdom, searching the floorboards for answers. At one point, I was afraid his brain would just malfunction and his eyes would sort of fall out of the sockets. Jüri thought and thought and did shots of *handsa* and thought some more. In the end, all my Estonian host could say was that summer is the best time to sauna, it is THE time to sauna, and that's why people sauna in summer. And I have to agree with him, summer is the best time to sauna.

It seems that sometimes the things that make no sense make the most sense of all.

That was after my family and Jüri's family had congregated in his smoke sauna in the sea-like fields of Setomaa. At first, I thought it was going to be a segregated sauna. Most saunas I've been in in Estonia have been segregated, so that women can discuss knitting and men can discuss car repair during their respective time allotments. So when Jüri's wife Janika and children and my wife and our children arrived after Jüri and I had been sweating and steaming for a good hour, I started to put my clothes back on. Jüri was swimming in a nearby lake and waved to the ladies as they entered the sauna. But when he got out, rather than getting dressed, too, Jüri brazenly reentered the sauna, wearing nothing except a stray leaf or snail.

"Hey, you can't go in there, my wife is naked in there!" I thought in protest. But the fact that my wife was in there didn't seem to bother Jüri at all. Like some kind of ancient man, Jüri thought that grunting and sweating next to some other guy's wife in a dark hot room was appropriate. At first, I was confounded, but I quickly decided that two could play at the sauna game.

"If that guy gets to sauna with my wife," I told myself, quickly dropping my trousers, "then I get to sauna with his!"

God, naked people are SO boring. With our clothes on, we all look rather intriguing, so it's such a disappointment to see that two other naked adults look basically the same as everyone else. This is a luxury that only I and those who have enjoyed a mixed sauna know because in the US, you usually don't get naked with your hosts after you eat dinner. Usually you sit around and complain about things with your clothes on. Then you shake hands or, if you've had a drink or two, hug and go home and watch TV.

Naked men look the most ridiculous. What do women see in us? We look like hairless apes carrying around a banana in front. Women are better but not much. Attractive when clothed, the child-rearing nature of the woman's body is most apparent in the nude. If men are hairless apes, then women are dainty cows. Their vast, udder-like breasts, alluring when restrained by colorful bikinis and braziers, are mostly unexciting when they are floating on the surface of a snail and leach-infested pond in the south of Estonia. In that context, nudity is all part of the scenery.

I thought these and other deep thoughts in the sooty smoke sauna where the smoke of the fire has rendered everything in its grasp black as space. I also pondered the carcinogenic properties of the smoke sauna, but one cannot openly criticize such a sacred place as being unhealthy, because the sauna is an institution with near religious significance in Estonia. One must not question its hidden power. One must simply obey and follow its unspoken rules.

In the smoke sauna that night, small children tossed ladles of water on the hot stones, dangerously close to the source of the heat. A few times I implored the youth to stay away from the treacherous red rocks, but was silenced by my naked guests who scoffed at my American paranoia. "Neeme is a good boy, a *tubli poiss*. He knows exactly what he's doing," said Janika of her ladle-happy, three-year old son. "He takes a sauna every day, you know."

Later, fully clothed, we sat around an old wooden table, drinking a strangely sweet concoction called "birch juice". I guzzled mine from an old ceramic cup that looked as if it had only been washed one time in 1968. The clear, mild "juice" was refreshing, but did not stay the questions gurgling around in my steam-shocked, foggy mind. "But if Estonians feel so comfortable getting naked in front of one another," I asked Jüri, "then why do they even wear clothes at all?"

This time Jüri sort of snorted and rolled his eyes. Then, with a small smile on his lips he said, "Justin, maybe you should just shut up and drink your birch juice."

I tilted the cup back and drank deep.

Climbing
Mount Everest

My Estonian language skills have been growing each day I've been back in Estonia. I understand a great deal of what is said around me. But once in a while, like some sort of free jazz, the Estonians slip into this mumbling language where I have absolutely no friggin' idea what they are saying.

For starters, Estonian conversations are usually barely above a whisper, and then there's the sucking in of the air once in a while when you say "jah". The radio, the TV, the newspaper—this can all be understood. But the actual conversations often come down to:

Mart: Jah, ulla ulla ulla ulla

Andrus: Ei, ma sala sala sala sala

Mart: Vist küll

(sarcastic laughter)

Are there actual words and sentences in those mumbles? It seems so.

While living in New York, still a city of immigrants,

I developed fairly perceptive ears. Two guys could approach me on the street and say, "Gabba gabba hey?" and I would respond, "Right, just hop on the J and get off at Delancey and Essex." I would think little of their accents. Jamaican, Korean, Kaliningradian—who knows and who has time to care?

Here in Eesti though, they just think I am hilarious. I went to visit Epp's Uncle Tiit the other night, a man who has infamously bad diction. While Uncle Toivo, usually lubricated by a few beers, has excellent diction and is a joy to listen to because I can understand every word, Tiit is a southern Estonian mumbler. Understanding what Tiit is saying is the linguistic equivalent of climbing Mount Everest.

Toivo would say, "Juu-stiin, kas sa tead, et sa räägid niiiii hääästi eeesti keeelt? Iiniimesed on elanud siiin uumbes 50 aaastat ja mitte üüks sõõõna!" (Justin, do you know that you speak Estonian very well? Some people have lived here for 50 years and can't say a word!") Tiit, meantime, would say something like, "J'n, t'd 't, s' r'g'd ni' h's'ti 'est' k'lt blub blub blub blub blub viiskend blub blub blub." (And supposedly it would mean the same thing) Even though these two wild and crazy guys have their own linguistic idiosyncrasies, they are still considered "normal". I, on the other hand, am abnormal.

"Justin, kas sul kitarri on?" ("Justin, do you have a guitar?") asks Ave-Liis, Tiit's daughter.

"Jah, on olimas," ("Yes, I do") I respond. It should be *olemas*, "O-leh-mas", but I said olimas, "O-lee-mas," by mistake; a slip of the tongue caught too late. This prompts a chuckle and a repetition of my mistake. "Ol-i-mas, ol-i-mas," she teases. I suddenly know how those poor first-generation Sino-Americans feel when they are ridiculed for substituting the letter "R" for the letter "L" and vice versa.

The other day at the department store, I engaged another acquaintance, whose cheeks grew equally rosy as I rattled through my accented words and awkwardly constructed sentences. [I use a lot of English constructions: "Have we met before?" is "Oleme kohtunud enne või?"] And then I crossed the boundary by wishing *Häid Jõule* [Merry Christmas], to which I received a terse "Jah" and a dry "suurepärane" [wonderful] in response.

I complain to Estonian friends, but they assure me that my language is just "*suurepärane*", [wonderful] and that they too have bad English accents (which is probably correct, though I don't notice their accents that often). And even if I say it right, I still get it wrong. I remember walking into a friend's place in Tallinn and exclaiming, "*Noh, kuidas su käsi käib!*" only to be met by reticent stares. "You didn't say anything wrong," my friend said later. "It's just the way you said it."

To keep climbing my own personal Mount Everest, I recently started reading an Estonian language book, Dagmar Normet's *Une-Mati, Päris-Mati, ja Tups*. And on every page there is a word I don't understand. But I still believe that Estonian isn't impossible. I am reminded of a college friend who studied Japanese. Night after night he worked into the late hours, just to memorize the alphabet! Now that was a difficult language. (And think of how difficult English actually is. Imagine trying to explain to a beginner the different meanings of sale, sail, seal, cell, and shell!)

Besides, learning Estonian gets me into all kinds of interesting situations. Like the time I went to obtain life insurance in Tartu. On the policy contract you are asked questions such as, *Kas Teil on diagnoositud HIV-viirust?* ["Have you been diagnosed with the HIV virus?"] That question I understood well enough to answer. Others were more complicated. One question I was asked by the agent was:

Kas olete teinud enesetapukatse?

This question bothered me because what I understood couldn't possibly be on an insurance form. That's because instead of what she asked, I heard:

Kas olete söönud enne hapukapsaid?

Literally, "Have you eaten sauerkraut before?" I thought about answering "*jah*" because we had *hapukapsad* for dinner the night before, but I decided that no matter how much Estonians like their *hapukapsad*, there's no way they'd ask you that in order to get an insurance policy. As far as I know, *hapukapsad* has no medicinal properties.

The agent then explained to me that *enesetapukatse* is when an *inimene* (person) *katsetab* (attempts) *tappa* (to kill) *ennast* (himself). Ah, *enesetapukatse*—suicide. *Kas olete teinud enesetapukatse?*—"Have you ever made a suicide attempt?"

I informed her proudly that I had never attempted suicide, and, to be safe, let her know that I had eaten sauerkraut on many occasions.

Some other foreigners in Estonia are spared such experiences because they have never bothered to learn Estonian. They have just decided to take themselves as tourists who have happened to extend their stay by months and years (and even decades). And yet there are plenty of foreigners who have mastered the language, who even get its strange little sayings.

One of my favorite of these sayings is *Nokk kinni, saba lahti*. Literally, it means that if your beak (*nokk*) gets stuck (*kinni*), then your tail end (*saba*) is exposed (*lahti*). But I needed a little more help in grasping this phrase's true meaning, so I asked a friend, who explained it to me: "Imagine that you are a bird. And imagine that you are somewhere, maybe on a hot roof. Your beak has gotten stuck in the tar, but your legs are still free." My friend actually acted this scenario out before my eyes. "You would like to get free, and so you tug and tug and tug until, bam, you get your beak free, but now you've lost your balance and your legs are stuck." Finally, he arrived at the point. "It means that if you focus too much on trying to solve one problem, you won't be able to take care of others as they happen." "Of course," I told him.

And I have been waiting for a good opportunity to use this very special Estonian saying ever since.

How I Learned
to Love Nastja

An Estonian friend recently moved back to Tallinn from abroad and complained to me, "God, I wish I had paid more attention in Russian class in school."

Man, that burned me up. Just the idea of it. Here we had an Estonian in the capital of Estonia lamenting her lack of Russian skills. It seemed to challenge the fundamental idea of the state, but also the relationship between majorities and minorities. I was from New York, where one could hear any language spoken. But everyone was supposed to be functional in English, and if they weren't, well, that was their own problem.

Not so in Estonia. Here people are more polite about such matters. And my friend didn't want to upset her neighbors, with whom I understand she has had some significant communication problems. Maybe there was a question about who takes out the trash, or where it would be possible to park one's car. Whatever the issue, the inability of one Tallinner to make herself understood to another Tallinner is frustrating to her.

Now, this friend is from Hiiumaa, the most Estonian place in Estonia. Had she grown up in Tallinn, she probably wouldn't have these communication problems. Just observing my other friends in Tallinn—those who probably never needed a Russian class—has enlightened me to their linguistic skills. They remind me of cartoon superheroes in a way. Their multilingualism is part of their secret identity. The way Bruce Wayne was a playboy by day and Batman by night, my friends can be Estonians to me but Russians to their neighbors. It comes as a surprise to me every time, to learn of an acquaintance's secret Russian talent. Everything is in Estonian, but when the lady down the hall asks a question about the plumbing, Katrin suddenly becomes Ekaterina and "Jah, jah, jah" becomes "Da, da, da".

For Estonians, such situations are what they call "normaalne". But they offended me in part, not only as an American who has read Mart Laar's history books, but as someone who had made an effort to learn the world's second smallest fully functional language.

"How the hell do you expect that lady to learn Estonian if you always speak to her in Russian?" I have said to more than one Estonian. But when I pester my Estonian friends about indulging their Russian neighbors' monolingualism, they usually shrug. Estonians relish efficiency, you see. They are more interested in getting things done than linguistic power politics, they say.

Still, I think there is actually more to it than that. There are hidden elements of compassion and fear in the Estonians' approach to communicating with their monolingual Russian neighbors. Compassion in that they feel bad that this great nationality should have to learn their small and unusual language, even to acquire a passport, and fear because of historical reasons, the way most of them arrived a few decades ago, and because the leader of their former mother country is a Judo-practicing former KGB man who nurtures a paranoid world view, and who would probably like nothing more than to see Mart Laar and the entire leadership of IRL in jail alongside Mikhail Khodorkovsky and Yulia Tymoshenko, on corruption charges, of course.

Living in Estonia, I acquired this mix of pity and fear for the local Russian community and maintained it. Until one fateful day at the supermarket.

On that day, my cart was full with Estonian produce, *küüslauguvõi*, *leib*, *mereväik*, and all the other wonderful things you people eat and drink. No, there was no *sült* (and there never is!). I was just about to unload my groceries at the checkout line, when an old man in a leather cap cut in front of me and started unloading his. I tried to flank him to regain my old slot in line, but he made some angry gestures with his arms and grunted what I took were some Russian obscenities at me and continued with his groceries. Of course, he managed to evince some pained beginner's level Russian from the stuttering Estonian cashier, and then he was on his way, another old asshole grunting and pushing his way into the abyss.

Something changed in me that day. Something hardened, something crystallized. I lost all of my compassion and all of my fear. What was left was pure self-centeredness, the same disregard for others that the Russian man in the supermarket had shown me, a true foreigner in his land. For years I had thought about Estonia's Russian "issue" and argued with wannabe intellectuals and propagandists on websites about official languages and citizenship laws. In all of my reading and arguing, I had hoped that I would happen upon a solution that would make every human being in the universe, or at least Estonia, happy. Why not adopt the European Charter for Regional or Minority Languages? Or why not ease citizenship requirements for certain groups? If it could keep meddling bureaucrats out of Estonia's affairs, and keep the local minority happy, then wouldn't it all be worth it, not to mention more Scandinavian-like and egalitarian?

But after that day in the supermarket, I just couldn't be bothered to care. I thought of all the nights I had spent with my notebook watching Andrus Ansip on the news and copying down his magnificent vocabulary, rewriting the words ten times so that they would stick in my mind. And then I thought of all those disenfranchised monolingual Russians in Tallinn watching Russian state-owned media and wondered if one of them had ever lost a second of sleep over the integration and accommodation of real newcomers to Estonia, people like me and Abdul Turay and João Lopes Marques and the many others who write columns about them who are living just next door. I thought of the asshole at the supermarket, cursing at me and bullying the checkout girl. I didn't care anymore if he had citizenship or spoke Estonian or felt at home in Estonia or was waiting for the Red Army tanks to return. He was on his own, as was I, in this little cold land.

Indifference. It's supposed to be the scourge of mankind, the very opposite of good Christian empathy. But in my case, it was liberating. It felt great. I would have opened the windows and sang, if it hadn't been so cold outside. A vast rock called the "Russian question" had been dislodged from my chest. And for the first time, Estonia's Russians stopped being a "question" or an "issue" or a "situation" to ponder or worry about and argue on the Internet about. All Estonian Russians became merely individuals to me, after that encounter in the supermarket. Some were upstanding citizens, some of them were assholes, but they were all different, and there was preciously little I could do about it either way. They were all just people living their lives, worthy of equal respect and courtesy (and intense disdain, if one happened to cut me off in the supermarket).

It was around this time that my first book came out, and it displaced a volume entitled *Selgeltnägija* by an individual named Nastja from the top of the bestseller lists. My friend told me in private that some Estonians were happy to see it happen, not only "because she's a Russian", but "because that witch has been number one for too long". This caught my interest. Who was this Nastja? What was that book about? Apparently, she really was a witch, but there are a lot of witches in Estonia. So, I think that her fame was at least in part due to her wholly non-Estonian image. And I have to say that I liked her. I liked the insolent look on her face on that book cover, her stormy eyes, her Frisbee-sized earrings. She was just so refreshingly...Russian, so different from the milquetoast Estonians I had to contend with day after day, a ray of light in the winter gray.

And yet she was also an Estonian, wasn't she? How could anyone challenge that? Nastja, as I found out much later, was competent enough in the language that I saw her laugh at some inside joke about men and reindeer antlers on a talk show. Not that I am a nationalist, but it always feels good when I see that someone else has wasted her time learning the second-smallest fully functional language in the world. And history and politics and communication troubles aside, I was really happy that someone like Nastja lived in Estonia. She made it much more interesting.

Tallinn,
Midwife of Fates

This is the story of two men, foreign men, men like me. One an American, the other an Australian, of whom I will share enough details so that to mutual acquaintances they shall be recognizable, but to the rest they will remain but characters on the bigger stage of the foggy city.

I am writing this in mid-autumn, it has been raining for days. There are wet leaves everywhere, every car is covered in muck and filth, the endless summer is deceased and buried, and we can only look forward to more cryptic murkiness. The darkness falls on everything like ravenous carnivores, in between every building and tree and sidewalk crack, so that even flashlights and headlights cannot penetrate it.

Tallinn sleepwalks along, limping through the slippery autumn leaves. And along its soggy streets walks Steve. His face bears its usual bemused look. His wife's lips are turned up though, puckered in a state of worry. Steve sees me and we stop and exchange formalities. Then I tell him that I know.

"I understand that you are in deep shit."

Steve looks a bit more bemused, though his eyes are steely, depthless, solid. They are the eyes of a man who has cried all his tears out a long time ago. "I'm being deported in eight days," he says and sighs.

"Eight days?"

"Eight days," he nods. His wife also nods behind him, her lips still pursed.

Our mutual Estonian friend gave me the rundown the night before. Steve forgot to count his days in country. Though he had secured an apartment in Kadriorg, a teaching position at a local college, he had neglected to file for a work permit in the allotted 90 days, and so upon visiting the local migration board office, was fingerprinted, photographed, and fined €350 for working illegally. Now he has to leave Europe and will require a visa to reenter, which is a shame, because Steve is a well-known writer, had plans of starting up a literary journal, he had connections, could have made a difference, could have made Tallinn the exciting, enticing gleaming jewel of a global city it has always yearned to be.

But Tallinn doesn't want Steve. It's tossing him out. I understand the legality of the situation, sure, yet at the same time I feel that Tallinn is missing a big opportunity. But that's just Tallinn! It suffers from myopia. Tallinn is too busy picking the lint from its navel that it neglected to install proper traffic signs. It's a self-centered city, a city that my friend Vello Vikerkaar describes as being stuck in a perpetual identity crisis. Too small to be important, too big to be obscure, it trudges forward through the eternal autumn of its life, wading through the wet leaves, dreaming of being cosmopolitan, but still tragically provincial.

In other parts of Estonia, it isn't so, says Vello. Tartu knows its place and Pärnu knows its place, he says. Even the farmers of Setomaa know who they are. But Tallinn is different, it's unpredictable, a freak electromagnetic force that could either pick you up and deposit you long distances away, like a tornado, or suck you down to the dark and lonely bottom of Lake Ülemiste.

The latter is happening to Arlo. While Steve packs his bags in Kadriorg, Arlo is unpacking his. On a late night this week, he arrived with his Estonian wife and children in tow from Australia. They have come to stay. I am not sure of the circumstances of the move. Maybe his Estonian wife made him an offer he couldn't refuse. Or perhaps he moved without much convincing. It happens. My Chilean friend Diego came to Tallinn months ago because he said it's a much better place to live than Santiago with its air pollution and poverty. He relishes Tallinn's smallness. "I can walk across town in 20 minutes. In Santiago, it would take hours to drive across town. Trust me, Tallinn is better." Maybe Arlo feels the same way.

Still, I worry for Arlo. I am sure that his family connections will earn him the proper documentation, but it's what comes after that isn't so easy. I've been living here for five years, speak the language fairly well, at least at a conversational level, and, let's not forget, my ancestors were also Europeans, so nobody glares at me when I walk down the street. But Arlo is different. His ancestors come from the Philippines. And his Estonian language consists of a few phrases.

Fortunately, he is moving to Tallinn and not to Viljandi. In Tallinn, you can get by as a foreigner. And yet you will always feel like a tourist. When the tourist season is over, though, people will glare at you because you are not from here. What I am worried about most is that Arlo will be dispatched to my door to hit me up for some insight or coping mechanisms. And I will have nothing to tell him other than he might as well put his trust in the hands of the city. It's the thing that brought him here. It should be the one to teach him how to manage.

Charisma Counts

When I first set foot on Estonian soil 10 years ago, the prime minister of this land was a man by the name of Siim Kallas.

I first saw him on the night of the parliamentary elections, where a new party called Res Publica had won big. But Siim didn't look upset at all. Instead he was swinging his hands back and forth and sort of half smiling/half grimacing to the TV cameramen, in an "Oh, gosh, isn't it embarrassing that you are filming me, but that's your job and this is my job, so, let's just pretend that I don't see you..."

I liked him immediately because, well, Siim Kallas is a peculiarly likable fellow. He is one of the chosen few who never age. Go back to those photos of Kallas from the IME project in 1987 and he looks exactly the same. He's even got the same dapper mustache, which would look odd on any other fellow, but seems to suit him. In fact, I am afraid to know what he looks like without it.

I caught Siim Kallas once at a Lennart Meri Conference where the moderator butchered his name, referring to the gentleman with the two i's as "Sim". "Sim this" and "Sim that". "What do you think about authoritarian capitalism, *Sim*?" I cringed every time he said it, but Siim (rhymes with scheme) didn't wince once. Instead he went on and on about something that I cannot remember but sounding very intelligent and using hand gestures that signaled his self-confidence to the audience.

After EU accession happened, I saw less of Siim. They said he'd flown away to Brussels to become a commissioner of something important and Tartu Mayor Andrus Ansip became the new face of the Reform Party and has been for many years, leading Kallas' political baby through two successful elections.

Yet Ansip's approval ratings are at an all time low these days. People are looking for alternatives. But Kallas, fortunately, has another baby, a biological one. And these days in Estonia her face is everywhere. Kallas' baby is not really a baby anymore. Her name is Kaja and she is 35 years old and she is very pretty. Of course, she has a sterling CV with accomplishments as a lawyer and businesswoman, ambition, intelligence, but she also happens to look really good, which is why magazines just can't help but make Kaja Kallas their cover girl. For weeks (months?) it seems that she has appeared on the cover of all printed material in the nation. The stories about her feed an intense public interest.

"Could she be Estonia's first female prime minister?" one tabloid even ventured to ask. Hmm. *Could she?* Even people who despise the current leader have confessed to me. "If she ran, I would vote for her because *she's just so pretty*."

And the problem is, recovering leftist that I am, if given the chance to vote for Kaja Kallas, I might vote for her too, for the same pathetic reason.

It's not the first time an Estonian female politician has tugged on my heart strings.

First there was Urve Palo, whose short skirt made me an ardent Social Democrat. Then, after the Center Party triumphed in municipal elections, and a very flattering photo of Kadri Simson and her big misty eyes appeared online, I suddenly found myself feeling sympathetic toward the Green Monster. "Maybe that Savisaar guy really *does* care about the poor and unfortunate people in Estonia," I caught myself thinking after seeing Kadri's picture. It was about that time that Marju Lauristin sprinted into my life. Yet it wasn't her eyes that did it for me. It was her brain. After spending an afternoon in one of her lectures, all I could think about was Lauristin. Lauristin, Lauristin. Lauristin, Lauristin. The way she rattled off statistics! And her passion for knowledge! Why, it was like a feverish dream. In fact, I was so impressed by Marju Lauristin's dynamic presence and intelligence that I became a Social Democrat again. Until I read another article about Kaja Kallas.

Fortunately for Estonians, I cannot vote. But my ability to be swayed by charismatic females sparked a new and interesting thought. Perhaps women voters are just as easily swayed by male politicians.

So *that's* the reason my mother keeps on buying all of Bill Clinton's books?

The thought that women might vote for male politicians because they like them in *that way* astonished me and led me into various unpleasant places. Were any of Estonia's male politicians attractive? Had it ever led them to electoral victory in the past? I wanted to know more.

Now, I am not the best judge of male attractiveness, but I can basically understand that Brad Pitt is better looking than, say, Elton John. But when it comes to Brad Pitt, Tom Cruise, George Clooney—well, they are all a bunch of dudes to me. And so are Estonia's male politicians. Toomas Hendrik Ilves, Siim Kallas, Edgar Savisaar, Andrus Ansip, Jürgen Ligi, Rein Lang, Juhan Parts, Jaak Aaviksoo, Ken-Marti Vaher, Urmas Paet. They all look slightly different from one another, but their appearances provoke an equal amount of disinterest in me.

But maybe for the women of Estonia it has been another story altogether. Maybe they voted for Siim

Kallas because of his fabulous mustache. Or Mart Laar because he was so round and cuddly. Or Andrus Ansip because the ladies of the land like to watch him cross-country ski.

Once when I asked a friend why she voted for Isamaa in 1992, despite having a pretty leftward social outlook, she blushed and told me, "But Isamaa had the handsomest candidates."

Isamaa was the party that set much of what has become modern Estonia in motion, selected, in part, on looks. Here, I have to ask—how much of history has been decided this way? Is that why Kennedy defeated Nixon? Or Obama defeated Romney? The ladies simply fancied the men who won more? We talk about politics, we talk about policies and statistics and polls. But the mysterious and paramount ingredient of the heart is ignored in these discussions. The political scientists write their columns and give interviews and provide expert analysis. They act as if the future will be decided on logical decisions and sound governance. But maybe a good chunk of what happens is actually up to a candidate's sporty physique or pretty blue eyes. In that case, you might as well let me vote in the next election. Don't worry. I promise I'll support the most convincing candidate.

Striving
for Perfection

There is an old Estonian saying, "Once we get going, we can't be stopped," and the same could be said of me, in any endeavor. I love traveling, and once I get traveling, I just want to keep on going, every few days a new hotel, a new city, more planes, trains, buses, boats, cable cars. When I get home I am disappointed. I don't know what to do with myself until the glow of traveling wears off.

Eating is the same for me, that insatiable appetite. Bring me a salad, bring me a main course, and dessert, and a few more drinks. Ah, yes, drinking, now that's a real disaster. One beer leads to another. By early morning, I don't want to remember, though I always do.

Some say I lack self-discipline, and I have to say that I agree, 100 percent. But I don't want to be this person. I dream of the perfect, balanced week, a week of measured consumption and regular exercise. I think we all dream of such a life, for this is the modern ideal, the image of what is the perfect person of our era.

Maybe for our grandparents the ideal person wore certain clothes and lived in a certain neighborhood and had a nice car, but we've taken it a step further: the ideal person of 2012 is so much more than clothes or possessions, he is everything, always working and yet always enjoying life to its fullest, always consuming delicious and exotic foods and beverages, and yet—most of all—always physically fit.

Here I am reminded of our dear friend Kaja who runs marketing for a telecommunications company, has six children, goes mountain climbing, and is remodeling her apartment in her spare time. Or our neighbor Janek, who manages a beverage company, goes on business sojourns to Japan, and makes sure to run around Lake Viljandi at every opportunity, even when it's minus 30 degrees Celsius outside, because Janek is smart, he has special clothes for running in Arctic temperatures, and special shoes for running on ice. This modern woman won't let work or home life keep her off mountain tops. This modern man will not let mere weather get in the way of his quest to fulfill his ideals.

I am jealous of people like Kaja and Janek and all the others who are in better shape than me. I tell myself that they are older, and that one day I might wake up and start running every day, eat only healthy foods, enjoy a good drink or two but know when to stop, work like a machine, read my children to sleep, surprise my wife with something romantic, and smile all the time, as any ideal person does, because regular exercise does wonders for the mind and so the ideal person is *always happy*.

But, alas, I am not there yet. I lack the self-discipline to see the project of "me" through, to master all elements of being an ideal modern human being, including getting in shape. While Kaja repels off of mountains and Janek charges up another hill, I am trying to convince myself to not eat that very delicious piece of pepperoni pizza, to not log in to my time-sucking Facebook account and instead go out for a jog, though I never find the time.

Years ago the English band Radiohead included a track on their seminal album *O.K. Computer* where a modulated electronic voice recited the words, "Fitter, happier, more productive, comfortable, not drinking too much, regular exercise at the gym (3 days a week), getting on better with colleagues at work…" Singer Thom Yorke called it the most depressing thing he had ever written, but I saw it as a satire of us, modern adults, and our ideal images of who we should be, happy people who work hard and then take off for luxurious holidays, where we can refresh our tans and take wonderful photos of our bodies in the sun to show everyone at home just how fit and perfect we are.

It's easy to be a mocker, and I am, but I also accept that without some ideal vision of who I should be, I would probably still be living with my parents. Early on in life, I developed my own idea of who the ideal person was, largely pieced together from my father's stories and books and Hollywood films. My ideal person was some kind of hybrid of an action hero and an artist, taking off for remote areas of the world where he got into memorable adventures and perhaps fell for a love interest before spinning the tales into fiction.

These ideals got me this far but, unfortunately, when I was developing my ideal self, I left out a few things. I forgot to code in moderation, and, especially, moderate, regular exercise, something I now yearn for, but never seem to find the self-discipline to attain. Like a lot of people, I see other people doing it every day, but can't find the will to just wake up and do it myself.

Here, I wonder about my friends Kaja and Janek. Maybe they were different. Maybe when they were children, they had different visions of who they would become. Maybe little Kaja had fantasies of mountain climbing. Or perhaps young Janek looked wistfully at the lake on extremely cold days, and dreamed of the day when he would run around it. But young Justin was too busy stuffing his face with pizza and watching Indiana Jones movies and now he can't manage to do what millions of other people do every day: get out of bed early and go for a run.

So now, later in life, I have to reprogram myself to fulfill these new ideals, so that I too can be "fitter, happier and more productive". And it's not just a matter of going down and running around the lake, because you know I'll wear the wrong shoes and overdo it (like everything else) and hurt myself in the process. No, I am going to need to do some research into proper foot attire and training methods, how many minutes to do it every day, what kind of terrain is most suitable for beginners. I've got to tackle this thing the way an ideal person would.

My friend in Belfast who is a runner says that it makes sense to go to a special shop where running shoes will be selected by a computer based on the shape of my foot and the way that I run. So, it's going to take some time. But, sooner or later, I am sure that my new ideal will be fulfilled—albeit it a moderate, perfect, 2010s kind of way. So watch your backs Janek and Kaja. Soon enough—I hope—I will be right behind you.

The Real Liis Lass

The waterfront of Shanghai glowed like ice cubes in fruit juices that night, its hundred-story commercial palaces piercing the air, the spectral ferries cruising by on the Huangpu River, giving all a haunted-Halloween-meets-Merry-Christmas feel.

"If you haven't seen the Bund, you haven't seen Shanghai," said Anneli. Anneli is an Estonian living in China. At the translation bureau where she works, they call her "silent blue" because she wears blue all the time and doesn't talk much. "You see these ferries, they only go back and forth," she said and laughed a little. "They're just part of the scenery, too."

We were going to walk to the event, but when she found out I hadn't seen much of Shanghai in my four days in the city, she said we would have to walk to the waterfront and then a take a cab. It was the night before I had to leave again, back to Beijing, then on to Berlin, Riga, and, finally, Estonia. Such is the life a globetrotting journalist.

The Bund surprised me with its glistening beauty and Anneli was right. If I had missed it, I really wouldn't have seen Shanghai. But the hostess of the meeting with Estonian readers that night surprised me just a bit more.

"We are going to the home of someone named Liis Lass," Anneli said, as she and her husband Christoph, an affable Belgian–German who works for a solar power company, accompanied me through the back alleys of the city, past the balconies and moonlight. "Have you ever heard of her?"

I nodded, but my stomach and heart sort of collided at the name. Not only had I *heard* of Liis Lass, you see, I had *read* all about her exploits in the stack of *Kroonikas* in our WC and even *seen* a few stills from her *Playboy* shoot. Those latter images filled my mind. Her long blonde hair. Her long legs. Her long...eyelashes. As Anneli knocked at the door, I tried my best to make these memories disappear and pretend that I had never heard of Ms. Lass nor had much interest in her at all.

Fortunately, Liis was very nice. She was taller than I expected and bounded around her very tastefully decorated apartment, and her friendliness helped to push those unfortunate memories of *Playboy* and *Kroonika* far into the depths of my mind, though I doubt anything could erase them completely.

The first two people I met inside were a Chinese woman, come to help cater the event, and a German student, who was tutoring Liis. Liis Lass is an actual person, you see, a person with a story, a person who studies German in her spare time. Before that moment in Shanghai, for me, she had been like most Estonian "celebrities", perpetually two-dimensional. She was from the pages from *Kroonika* and *Playboy* and that's where she would stay. But that person in the magazines is not the real Liis Lass.

The real Liis Lass was apparently there before us that night in Shanghai. She sat on the couch between Anneli and Tõnu, a factory manager who told me about the art of making fresh *verikäk*.

The Liis I met that night was very entrepreneurial and inquisitive. She said she was some kind of fashion emissary, while she wasn't running her music studios in Tallinn and Beijing. Her recent home countries included South Korea and Japan. She planned on staying in China until she moved to Singapore to pursue a business career. But before that, she had to go to North Korea. "I read a really interesting book about North Korea," she said, "I just have to see what it's really like."

And the more I came to know the real Liis Lass, by drinking with her, eating pizza with her, speaking with her and listening to her, the more I realized that I was dealing with a fairly complex human being haunted by her past as an Estonian socialite. "So you managed to escape from Estonia," I joked to her. Well, you could say it was a joke. She nodded and smiled and said, "I'm not sure if I'm ever going back." I also felt tremendously guilty for reading about her social life in *Kroonika* and for pausing to look at those nude spreads (even though she's the person who agreed to the photo shoot, right?). I felt dirty, like an intruder, as if I had read her diary. And I vowed that night to never think I knew another person from reading their book or about them in a magazine again. It just didn't seem fair.

Don't judge a book by its cover. What a hackneyed statement! And yet the cliché resonated with me.

"You know, I feel like I already know you," Anneli and Christoph said later as we hailed a taxi. "After reading your books, it seems like you are an old friend." They both studied me to see if I really was that man from the books. Maybe they decided that I was, or that I was someone entirely different.

"So, what did you think of Liis Lass?" I asked them instead.

"She seemed very intelligent," Anneli said after some thought. "And more beautiful in person."

Months later, I saw Liis again on the cover of the latest issue of *Kroonika*. It was in the supermarket in Viljandi. I was pushing a cart filled with toilet paper and she was in her high heels standing on a balcony overlooking the Bund, a young Estonian singing the praises of a new life in trendy Shanghai.

I didn't bother to read the article though. It didn't interest me.

America's Business

At the airport in Helsinki, the luggage carts were free. They were as free as the chairs; as free as the toilets. At the airport in Vancouver, the carts were free; as free as the view from the windows; as free as the napkins at the airport cafés. But at the airports in New York and San Francisco, the carts for your luggage cost $5.

That's right, you get off a plane—hot, sweaty, jet-lagged. You wait to go through customs. You stand among your fellow travelers, hopeful that your bag made it to your destination with you. And then, after you lug it off the baggage carousel, you swagger on over to the line of carts, dig out your credit card, and provide a few measly dollars from your savings so that you can use it. This is America, after all; and America's business is making money off of you.

I paid it, of course. But I felt a little dirty. Canadians and Finns were getting things for free that I, as an American, had to pay for. Sure, it was only $5. But in Canada it was free. In Finland it was free. Why is it free there, but not here? I just don't understand.

At the hotel where I stayed in San Francisco, I became increasingly paranoid. The food in the room was hooked up to sensors that went off when you removed an item. I didn't find out about this until I located a small booklet that warned me of the perils of eating a Snickers bar in a San Francisco hotel. It would cost me $4 plus sales tax and a 20 percent restocking fee to eat said bar. Therefore, candy I bought across the street for less than $1 could wind up costing nearly ten times that in my hotel!

After I discovered that the candy bars cost $7.50, I became worried that other things were not free. Maybe there was a special charge for flushing the toilet, or even turning on the TV. Maybe I would go to check out and find out I had watched TV for 15 minutes at $4 per minute. I am sure it was written in fine print somewhere in my room. TV+San Francisco real estate prices = big fees, right?

But since I am smart (or at least very cheap), I hatched a plan. At the little Arab-owned and operated convenience store across the street, I bought a new Snickers bar for 75 cents to replenish my hotel minibar. There were sensors in the minibar that reported to the front desk when an item had been removed, but I would just say my baby daughter had played around with the candy and I had put it back. Because there was no way that I was going to pay four dollars plus sales tax and restocking fee for candy! It was against my principles. After the baggage cart fee, I had reached my limit.

Inside the shop across the street, the clerk was watching a French film from the 1950s dubbed in English. This calmed the hatred that was burning up inside me about the American candy bar.

"This country is actually pretty cool," I thought to myself. "Arab guys watching French film noir while guys like me buy Snickers bars? That doesn't happen in Estonia every day."

But the Arab film aficionado wasn't alone in the store. There was also an Asian guy with a goatee and an Obama '08 T-shirt. The fog covered the buildings outside and rolled up and down the hilly streets. And on the counter, under a panel of glass there was money from all different countries. Mexican money. Malaysian money. And there, representing Europe, was a five-kroon note. At this I proudly whipped out my 25-kroon bill featuring Estonian national writer Anton Hansen Tammsaare and displayed it to the clerk. His eyes lit up when he saw the currency.

"Are you from Estonia?" he asked.

"No," I responded. "But my wife is."

"Do you know who that is?" he tapped at the note beneath the glass.

"Sure. It's Paul Keres, the chess player."

The clerk looked me in the eyes. "Keres was very famous. Veeeerrrrry famous!"

I paid for my chocolate and was on my way. But I for once felt immensely proud of the country of my birth. Here it was, the big cultural melting pot, a place where Arab store clerks watched French films and collected Estonian money in a city founded by Spanish missionaries. Annoying fees for luggage carts and overpriced candy bars aside, it was hard to get any more inspiring than that.

Drug Wars and
Flying Couches

"And he puts his cocaine in the microwave. I mean, who does that?" Los Angeles, Los Angeles. It's such a ridiculously stupid city. People would rather spend hours in traffic than get behind some kind of comfortable and effective public transportation scheme. And I am one of these people. I am one of these people sitting at a table in an Ethiopian restaurant hearing about the exploits of an entertainer with a $500-a-day cocaine habit. "There were lines going everywhere. I mean here, there, on everything."

I like stories like this because it makes me feel as if I am rather normal, like I've made out OK in the stinky stanky tarpits of life. I've never even done lines. I credit Melle Mel's "White Lines (Don't Do It)", but also just the idea of doing an expensive, addictive, and often life-threatening drug doesn't make sense to me. It's like heroin. Let's count the casualties. And this is something you will pay to do?

Hell yes. South of the border a drug war is ongoing. In fact, it's now referred to as The Drug War, so as not to be confused with The War on Drugs. As it was explained to me at the Ethiopian restaurant, the armies of the drug lords are stronger and more effective than those at the disposal of the central government. The enemies are carved into pieces. When they recently found a human head in a plastic bag near the HOLLYWOOD sign, it was thought at first to be related to Mexico's drug war, though it's more likely some local out to get national attention (and they all are). Should demand for Mexico's wares diminish in the *Estados Unidos*, the revenue base of the drug lords would no doubt decline. But until then, more heads and hands and feet, more entertainers with $500-a-day cocaine habits, more traffic.

The Ethiopians eat with their hands. Their beer isn't half bad either. Better than Saku, not as good as A.Le Coq, easier on the gut than those jars of brown stuff the Setos sell from the back of their cars during the *Setokuningriigi Päevad*.

One downside to knowledge of the Estonian tongue is the inability to speak about Estonia without using Estonian words or expressions. Like *Setokuningriigi Päevad*. It translates as "Seto Kingdom Days". But that just sounds clumsy and awkward. How else could you say it? "Days of the Seto Kingdom"? Just as bad. How about Viljandi *Paadimees*, the "Viljandi Boatman"?

That also sounds odd to my ears. And it doesn't matter how you translate it, because Seto Kingdom Days and Viljandi Boatman don't mean anything to anyone outside of Estonia because nearly all people on Earth are unaware of the existence of the Seto people, let alone their kingdom, and they have never heard of Viljandi, and therefore are completely ignorant of its mystical Boatman!

They do know about *kaksteist kuud*. This means "twelve months" in Estonian, but is interpreted by English-speaking ears as "cocks taste good". Everyone knows about kaksteist kuud. Go to some small Polynesian island and raise the blue, black and white flag of the Estonian republic and you'll see the little naked children throng the shores shouting out, "Kaksteist kuud! Kaksteist kuud!" They've all seen the YouTube clip where the smarmy backpackers get pretty Estonian girls to say it over and over again.

Listen, even at the lowest points of my sad and alcoholic pre-marital life I did not stoop to the levels of these YouTube clip-uploading *cafoni*. *Cafone* is a southern Italian dialect word. It means a disreputable or ill-mannered person. I was once called this by an older person when as a teenager I ordered three hamburgers at lunch. But now I am calling you all out. It's time to let it go. Just as MTV retired "Ice Ice Baby", it's time to retire kaksteist kuud.

But you know they won't let it go. No one will. Our

friend recently was injured in Viljandi. She was walking down the street when someone dropped a couch on her head from a second-floor window. Just a minor concussion. But still! Our friend was hit in the head by a couch. I don't know why some part of me still believes life could be some other more rational or sane way. Couches falling from the sky. Microwaved cocaine. *Kaksteist kuud.* When the plane landed in New York it was snowing. Our driver was an old man, half my height. We listened to Dean Martin or Frank Sinatra all the way home. "Papa loves mambo, Mama loves mambo..."

People keep inviting me to all kinds of events. One journalist wants to interview me about jealousy in relationships. Someone wants me to give a presentation at an assembly of Estonian teachers on the local education system. Sometimes I would just like to scrap it all and start playing João Gilberto tunes in some club somewhere. Or even Dean Martin. I could sing like Dean Martin. At this point, why not? In a way, it makes perfect sense.

Estonian House

What did I expect from Los Angeles? Brad Pitt, Angelina Jolie, hot dogs, Ice Cube, Venice Beach, Big Kahuna burgers, guitar solos, Emilio Estevez, gin and juice, rollerblades, the OJ Simpson trial, afros, boob jobs, Michael Jackson's doctor, Melrose Place, Liz Taylor's dead husbands. What I got was a lift to the Los Angeles Estonian House courtesy of an Estonian woman with a Pakistani name.

By that point, I was afraid I had completely forgotten the Estonian tongue, but it came back to me with Saima, rushing in, and it occurred to me what a peculiar thing it is to know more than one language. I've been on a book tour for most of this year, and I agreed to present at the LA *Eesti Maja*. It's in a single-story, pueblo-like structure in one of the city's neighborhoods, and neighborhoods are the skeleton key to understanding Los Angeles, but I can't remember in what LA neighborhood the Estonian House is situated.

Something something "Hills" or "Park" or "Heights" maybe.

Inside, it was like the New York Estonian House, the dim lighting, the flags, the portraits of Johan Laidoner and Konstantin Päts, Lennart Meri and Toomas Hendrik Ilves. "Rüütel didn't send us one," a gentleman said to me. Then the dolls in national costume, the choirs, the Saku beer, the imported issues of *Kroonika* with the photos of national "celebrities" and their love lives. The Estonian press is so starved for material you can tell them almost anything and they'll report it. Faux Esto Celebrity: "I don't feel well today. Maybe something I ate. Can we do the interview tomorrow?" Estonian Tabloid: "Faux Esto Celebrity Ill!" Stranger on Los Angeles Street Approaching Faux Esto Celebrity Clutching Imported Estonian Tabloid: "Hey, *esse*, are you feeling OK? I read you were sick, bro."

Yes. It's a pity I haven't joined forces with the Estonian comedy troupes, even just to heckle them, because by now all book tours basically become stand-up comedy routines. The return of Seinfeld. Cue the popping, synthetic bass lines. Cue Kramer. Cue Newman. I ramble on about the foundation of the publishing house, the struggle to finish a book—and it's my first book, OK—but the audience doesn't want to hear that, they want to hear funny stories about meat jelly. "It's clear and it jiggles and it has something in it. They tell me it's 'meat and it's delicious'. I ask, 'What kind of meat is it?' and then I ask, 'From what part of the animal?'" "That's good," they roar. "Now tell us about blood sausage!" And I tell them.

Estonians are so polite. I am afraid to cuss in front of them for fear that they might blush. And, you know, a lot of them are quite short, sturdy and round: the little people. Maybe the Hobbit comparisons aren't off their mark. I really like when an Estonian is even taller than me, someone like Jaak Aaviksoo, you know, and you talk, and the Estonian leans in to hear, just to let you know that they may wear ties now, but their forefathers carried battle axes. It is in the midst of the polite Estonians that I become acutely aware of my Mediterranean hilltop peasant roots, dirt that cannot be scrubbed free. What do these singing elephants think of me? My neighbor in Estonia thinks my last name is "Preatone". Epp's cousin thinks our family name is "Pizza".

Ah, and here's the calendar I've been waiting to see, the one with the photos of Estonians in military uniform, Nazi German military uniform. It hangs innocently on the wall and I suppose there is nothing wrong with it, to those who will listen, except the conscripted soldiers are smiling like they actually are having a swell time under foreign military occupation. "It was a great time," they seem to say. "They gave us these cool uniforms, neat guns, three square meals a day."

There's something very hazy and peculiar and Los Angeles about the scenes in the 20th Waffen SS commemorative calendar though, like they really shot the photos somewhere up in the smog of the Hollywood Hills instead of at Sinimäe.

The Estonians don't talk about the calendar though. They offer you food, they offer you beer, they offer you coffee, they want to talk about languages and lives and the coming of the euro. Everyone is so polite. Why are they so polite to me? I look around at the faces in the room and the people all look so similar, the Uralic eyes, the Teutonic ears. They are all related, they've been together for a long, long time. From the marshlands to the mesas, from the *Läänemeri* to the Pacific Ocean. And this is the end, the last stop on their long trek. There is nowhere else to go. The kids speak Estonian, but the grandkids? But they are unfazed by it. They soldier on with their calendars and cookbooks and imported issues of *Kroonika*. I tell them I am disappointed in LA. I was expecting to see Angelina Jolie.

"Don't worry, I'll go call her," a polite Estonian gentleman says to me and walks out of the room. "Angelina will be right over."

An Estonian
Girl in New York

Liis was unhappy. She had seen most of what Midtown Manhattan had to offer: Times Square, Fifth Avenue, and Broadway, and within it, Macy's, Toys 'R' Us, Tiffany's, and FAO Schwartz. But something was missing. On the second floor of New York's largest toy store, surrounded by obscenely sized teddy bears and Harry Potter merchandise, she confided in me: "I want to go back to Forever 21."

Forever 21. For this teenage Estonian girl from Tartu one particular clothing store beckoned with its glistening escalators, booming dance music, flashing lights, elegant wardrobes, and ensemble cast of hundreds of blazed European tourists, ladies who were willing to spend to the bottom of their purses to capture a little bit of New York class in a bag. Liis is not yet 16, so 21 seems infinitely distant. As our babysitter in Estonia, she had saved for months and months just to come to Manhattan, just so that she could step foot in a place like Forever 21.

When Liis first saw the lights of New York from our car window on the way home from the airport, she was both awed and tremendously satisfied. "It's so beautiful," she cooed. And then, "My best friend Kaisa is just going to die of jealousy when I tell her about it. She is going to cry, cry, and cry some more!" There was no empathy in Liis' voice. She was very content that she would be the first of her friends to see Manhattan. She had told us that the girls at her school in Tartu would gaze upon her with adoration and respect once they heard that she had been shopping in New York.

While Kaisa has no doubt drenched her sheets in envious tears by now, Liis obtained for her a consolation prize: a $30 Rolling Stones shirt acquired in Times Square. Liis spent an equal sum on a Beatles T-shirt, and then $10 for five "I Love NY" T-shirts for various friends. I thought this was the zenith of this young Estonian woman's fevered spending frenzy. I was wrong. On the way back to Forever 21, we stopped inside another delectable spender's paradise, this one called Strawberry. One T-shirt inside proclaimed its values. "I want clothes, money, boys, fame, candy, and good grades," it read. I could only spend about thirty seconds in the place before I excused myself to walk around the block.

I had been amused by Liis' shopping antics but also touched in some way. In New York, she seemed

Justin Petrone

267

amazed by everything: the battered Subway lines, the glossy skyscrapers, the pulsing neon lights. Even the Empire State Building excited her. I had seen these things so many times, they had become like wallpaper to me. With Liis they came back to life. In Strawberry, though, I reached my limit. I was done with it in half a minute. She spent half an hour there. Why? What kind of person could spend so much time in a store filled with dresses and shoes?

The obvious answer: a woman. A woman like Liis, like my wife Epp, like my mother. When I was a little boy, my mother would take me to places like Strawberry. I would scan its interior, searching for something mildly interesting. Sometimes I would think I would see toys shimmering in the distant corners of the clothing store, only to be disappointed when I discovered the "toy mirage" was really just more shoes and bags. To pass the time, I would hide among the clothing racks to torment my mother. Only when the son had disappeared for a while would she even notice his absence. She was always irritated when I popped out from behind a brassier to cry, "Peak-a-boo!"

Maybe such episodes built up my tolerance for places like Strawberry. It's true, I had matured since those days, warily accompanying Epp to shops to answer such probing questions as, "What do you think of this shirt?" Or, "Do you think this bag would go with my winter coat?" On such excursions, I usually just say, "Yes," or, if I am feeling honest, "I don't know." I am generally useless, but don't mind carrying an extra bag around or opening the door.

When Liis finally emerged from Strawberry, shopping bags dripping from every arm, I was relieved. "Thanks for waiting," she feigned an exhausted smile. "Um, I don't think we need to go to Forever 21 anymore," she blushed. "I spent all my allowance."

Epp later rejoined us after doing an interview for a book with an actress in Times Square. Liis had wanted to go uptown to the Dakota to see where John Lennon had been shot, but our group voted for Union Square where there was an organic farmers market and, for my purposes, a Virgin Megastore where I could hide out while the Estonians raided another hall of consumer goods.

It was now early evening, and everyone was beat from walking and shopping. Even Liis' Strawberry afterglow had subsided. She didn't need any more clothes; she needed a pillow. As we ascended the Subway stairs into the bustling, sunny square, though, her tired eyes fixed on several large signs. There was a Strawberry here, too, she noticed, and a DSW, where they sold discount shoes! And right between them, sparkling in the summer light, was a Forever 21.

"I can give you the rest of your allowance today," Epp chirped as Liis rifled through her wallet.

"You will?" Liis guffawed.

"Isn't New York fun?" I patted Liis on the shoulder. She didn't answer, but from the mad gleam in her eye, I could see that she was once again very, very happy. But she wasn't the only one. As if diving into an Olympic-sized swimming pool, Epp swooned into DSW to try on new pairs of shoes. I waltzed over to the music store to explore the sounds of Jamaica, Nigeria, Brazil. For me, going to the music store has always been like going on a round-the-world trip, or sometimes a voyage back in time, or to the future. Music takes me places, it adds meaning to my life. But where can a dress take you? What meaning can a pair of shoes give to your life?

"I have my own theory," Epp informed us as we waited later for a subway train. "Using our hands helps us to relieve stress. Our grandmothers sewed and made their own clothes. But to release tension nowadays, women go shopping instead." I pondered the therapeutic benefits of shopping as our train shot us under Manhattan. And, at one stop, I caught a glimpse of a very tired Liis softly stroking her new bag.

Wild Weather

The morning after we got back I went to unearth the car. It was like an archaeological dig or one of those drilling endeavors in the Arctic. "Judging by these ice cores, an asteroid hit Earth 65 million years ago."

The vehicle was buried under a good foot or more of snow. Because there had been a thaw while we were gone, a layer of ice had formed in between the layers of snow. It took me two hours to get the car clean using a shovel and a brush.

I borrowed the shovel from my neighbor. When he came out, lighting a cigarette, blue circles beneath his eyes, I inquired as to why all the snow in the parking lot had been pushed behind my car.

"You were gone for a long time," he grunted, smoking. "We thought you had emigrated or something." Then he added, "The weather has been wild this winter." Actually, he used the word *metsik*, which translated in my jet-lagged brain to "foresty" as *mets* means "forest". "The weather has been foresty this winter," he seemed to say.

Then I saw his domestic partner/girlfriend/wife/ just friend (who knows in this country) and wished her a very big and boisterous "Tere hommikust!" to which she replied with a very anemic "Tere hommikust!" and looked me in the eye for about a nanosecond. I was afraid I had startled her. I felt as if I had been too forthcoming with my "Tere hommikust!" It occurred to me then that I was back in Estonia.

When the girls got back, the first thing they did was put on the stereo, which still had a Christmas music disc in it. Estonian children's music. It had some kind of funky organ combo backing a chorus of little kids singing about snow being on the ground and birds going south—*linnud läinud lõunamaale*—and there was something so psychedelic about the recording. Estonian children's music is nutty. It's also taken very seriously. There's even a TV program called *Laulukarussel* where children sing songs and TV viewers vote by mobile phone for the singers they like best.

I attribute this to an odd form of masochism on the part of the adults. Their way of humiliating the children into obedience is to get them to sing complex, ridiculous songs, wearing silly national costumes. "Now, Krõõt, if you want a cookie, you'll have to sing *Radiridirallaa, pagane on valla* three times and sing it like you mean it!" Or "Joosep, if you want any Christmas presents this year, then repeat after me":

Taba-taba-taba-taba-taba-tabatinna.

Taba-taba-taba-tamm, taba-taa.

Laba-laba-laba-laba-laba-labakinnas

Üks sula, kaks sula, talv on hea.

Talv on hea translates as "winter is good". And isn't it? I was hoping for all the snow to melt, but then I remembered that when the white stuff is gone, that just means it will start raining again. Hmm, snow or rain? What will it be? Maybe snow is good in this regard. Maybe the children's song is right.

At night, I shared a cup of coffee with my foreign Estonian friend and commiserated. "How does it seem to you just being back?" my friend asked. "Estonia, I mean."

"It's so quiet here," I told him. "All I see from my window is the lake and woods."

"I feel it every time," he said. "Even going from Helsinki to Tallinn. Estonia seems so sleepy."

"I said 'good morning' to my neighbor this morning and I think I frightened her," I confessed to my foreign Estonian friend as we drank coffee. "I forgot that people are a little shy around here."

"Oh, I gave up saying 'good morning' to the neighbors a long time ago," he said, sipping his coffee. "If they make eye contact with me, then I usually just say, 'Tere.'"

Exile on
Tallinn Street

I am a foreigner here. I am many other things, but this is my chief designation in the eyes of society. This is perhaps the situation of anyone who is a foreigner anywhere. Now I regret all the times I inquired as to the source of a person's accent in the US. "And where are you from? The former Yugoslav Republic of Macedonia?"

Foreigner. This is not necessarily a burden. It lifts you above the others, singles you out from the pack. Anyone can be a writer, but not everyone can be a *foreign* writer. Anyone can play guitar, but not everyone can be a *foreigner* playing guitar. Some of Estonia's most successful musicians are foreigners: see Dave Benton or Ruslan Trochynskyi from Svjata Vatra. Anyone who's seen Ruslan yield his scythe and croon in Ukrainian remembers him for his foreignness. But who are the guys backing him up? Ah, just a bunch of Estonians. So, there you have it. Foreigners are special. When you walk down the street, my fellow foreigners, hold your heads up high!

And yet, just as being a foreigner sets you apart from the rest of Estonian society, it also makes you invisible. Conversations typically revolve around language acquisition or reactions to the local cuisine. Few people really talk to you about anything important, because few people really know how to talk to you. Whole conversations cascade around you in which you can play little role, maybe because you don't understand everything being said, but mostly because you have so little to contribute. I recently watched two acquaintances have a deep conversation about forestry. Forestry! What do I know about forestry? Even if we were speaking the same language, we'd be speaking different tongues.

This was an issue in my second book. Most of the main characters, the deep characters, the ones who carried around with them meaning, were foreigners. The Estonians were like cardboard cutouts of people, two-dimensional, but not only for my lack of ability to translate them into text, but because so few of them had shared any shred of their souls with me. This was perhaps less because of the national character of the Estonian people, than because of the simple fact that I was an outsider, a foreigner, and somehow disconnected from the reality around me. Being a foreigner gives one the unique ability to walk down the street in one land, and still simultaneously, metaphysically, be in another.

Not like it would be any better there. I feel the same claustrophobia around most of my countrymen. Just as Estonia is too quiet, America is too loud. When I arrive home in New York, I snake through the sweaty bowels of John F. Kennedy International Airport, only to cross through the gates of US customs, where I am always made to feel as if I have done something wrong, though at last check, I have committed no crime. I get nervous standing there, wondering if my name has somehow wound up on some kind of list. "No Teen Idols!" "But I'm not Timberlake, I'm not Bieber!" "Guards, take him away!" "I swear, hey, what are you doing? Get your hands off of me! I'm innocent! I can't even dance, watch me, I'll prove it to you." "Mmm. Resisting arrest? That's another 10 years." "No, no, there must be some mistake!" "Tell it to your lawyer, kid."

America. The over-saturation of stimuli, the clamor of the crowds, the thousands of TV sets suspended from the ceilings blaring the day's misfortunes, pundits yelling over one another, people climbing over each other, the aroma of fried chicken and pizza, old newspapers, Andean flute players, Penn Station, New York City! One never feels so alive as when he's cruising the subway standing next to some punk Wall Street broker with a flattop who is singing along to The Supremes on his iPod. *"You can't hurry love. No, it just has to wait..."*

And when you finally emerge from the swampy mess, battered and chafed, and you land back in Estonia, you exhale. I feel this every single time I make the journey between the two countries. The heat of America, the coolness of Estonia. The more I think about it, the more it reminds me of the Estonian sauna, running between the oven-like conditions of the *saun* to the ice waters of the lake, only to find peace somewhere in between for a few fleeting moments.

Just as the Americans annoy me with their 24-hour cable news networks, the Estonians annoy me because they don't know how to live, they don't know how to enjoy themselves. I've watch construction workers slave late into the evening, 10, 11 o'clock at night, cigarettes dangling from their lips, blue circles beneath the eyes. There is this incredible urgency to everything they do, because summer only lasts so long, and soon it will be too cold to work anymore. I am sure that it all makes sense, but at the same time I feel that they are committing suicide, that never-ending work and drink and smoke are the Estonian version of *harakiri*.

I cannot change anything though. I cannot advocate a *mezzogiorno* for my neighbors. I cannot organize one for myself. Could you imagine in Estonia stopping work at around 1 pm to rush home and eat a prolonged, savory meal until about 5 in the evening, lounging around, munching on olives and fennel and telling pointless jokes and stories? No. It just wouldn't happen here. In Estonia, there must be moving, doing, consuming... The more I think about it, I don't fit into America or Estonia or anywhere. I have become a perpetual foreigner. I will be a foreigner everywhere I go.

The Missionary
Position

There is no reason to feel bitter today. The weather is
gorgeous. Not a cloud in the sky. The huge mounds
of dirty snow are melting. At lunchtime, I went for a
walk around Viljandi, took in the lake, the winding
old streets, the proud, renovated homes that gleam in
the sun and the shanty-like dumps that still stand beside them looking as if the Germans only retreated
yesterday.

Is winter really over? In my heart I don't believe it
is, but the weather and the calendar say it is so. I had
resigned myself to an endless winter, Antarctica until
the end. It's been months since I succumbed to the
cold. And now it's suddenly mild? And I am just supposed to forget about all that?

But I must adjust. I have no control over the weather just as I have no control over the condition of Viljandi's houses or sidewalks. Estonia just is what it is
and I strongly suspect that I will be unable to change
it in any meaningful way. How could I? I am just one

man, and certainly not gifted with the self-confidence or spiritual fortitude to join the ranks of Dr. King or Gandhi, both of whom were assassinated, I'll add. No, I'm just a puny individual. OK, so I may be a little taller than most, but so what?

Just as I succumbed to the Estonian winter and now spring, I have come to accept that I am not going to wean the drunks at the A ja O off the bottle. I am not going to stop your cousin from blowing his salary at this country's fleet of casinos. I am not going to make your waitress perkier, or neuter your neighbor's cat so that your property doesn't smell like a dance club urinal. I am not going to "integrate" the Estonian Russians or tame the vehicular insanity of the Tallinn–Tartu highway. How am I supposed to change Estonia? I can't even vote.

Yet, the impression I get from friends and acquaintances is that many foreigners think that they can somehow change Estonia. That it would be easy, simple, if only everyone listened to them. Moreover, it seems as if some are frustrated that Estonians haven't listened more attentively to their exceptional and brilliant ideas. It is my observation that when we so-called "Westerners" come to Estonia, we often fall into the trap of assuming this "missionary position". The attitude is based on the belief that one has come from a superior culture and that the same person is therefore entitled to lecture the locals about the "proper" ways to do things to make the inferior culture more like the superior one.

I admit, I have done the very same thing here, over and over again. How many times have I raged and ranted against, say, Estonian sexism? It seems I am the only one in this land troubled by the fact that there is but one female minister in the current government. For most Estonians, it's *normaalne*. Not for me though. I still believe in the equality of the sexes, which means out of 12 Estonian ministers, six should ideally be women, even if we haven't elected a gal president of the United States yet. But it should be easier in Estonia. This is the new Europe, a land of efficiency, prosperity and progress, the e-*riik*. Here one should be able to simply push a button and get a female prime minister. Just like that!

I'd like to think that such issues are unavoidable and probably not just a symptom of the imaginary West–East or American–European divide. Estonians who find themselves confronted by the peculiarities of any given country also tend to gripe. "What, no free Internet?" "Paper checks? You guys are still using these old-fashioned things?" "You still have a landline?" "This bread is terrible." "What do you mean they don't sell kefir at the store?" Still, I doubt that any of these Estonians actually thought that by writing a well-intended blog post or commenting anonymously on an online news story, or just bitching to their friends, that they could change things.

Anyway, I've decided to give up my missionary work. I don't feel like doing it anymore, and I don't think that the Estonians have ever taken one of us American "missionaries" seriously.

Often, I think back to America. Fifty years ago I might have had the cultural firepower to go around bragging about my shining city on a hill, where the plumbers live right next to the doctors, but these days the doctors live beyond tall fences, down long driveways, far removed from the plumbers, who may or may not be citizens. And don't ask me. As I write these lines, sixty-three percent of Americans think our country is heading in the wrong direction. It is the majority opinion.

Every country has its problems, but it seems to me that some of us "Westerners" still believe in the illusion that solving Estonia's problems should be simpler. Maybe it was the foreign ministry's "positively transforming" slogan that gave them that idea, or maybe because they have seen Estonia transform positively, but that kind of transformation will never happen with the snap of some American or British or German's fingers.

I have learned from living in a small Estonian town that changes happen on a much smaller scale. Take Viljandi's Old Town, for example. It will take time, but I am sure that at some point in the future, most of the houses will be renovated. Still, there will be those dwellings that remain uncared for, and just might be demolished altogether. Can I contribute? Sure, I can only take a paint brush and paint my own house. Sometimes that's all you can really do to make a change in the world.

Those Hot-Blooded
Estonian Women

Estonian women, what are they like? This question reminds me of an American judge who once famously said that while he couldn't provide a legal definition of pornography, "he knew it when he saw it." And I feel the same way about Estonian women. I can't tell you exactly what they are like, but I know one when I see one.

It happened just yesterday that my Swedish friend Erland related to me his encounter with a pretty seller at a café. "There was something about her, you know," he said, his eyes distant, as if we were two sailors on the deck of a ship. Erland smiled. "She was just so firm."

But he didn't mean that she was firm in form—in good shape in other words—though she certainly is. He meant that she was serious, austere, sober. The seller stood up straight, spoke when spoken to, and maintained moderate eye contact. Any conversation that passed between Erland and the seller had to do with the business at hand, and there was no trace of irony or humor in the seller's actions. Instead there was something very eastern in the seller's demeanor, like one of Bruce Lee's karate kicks tracing a silent, fluid path through the air.

"She was an Estonian," I told Erland. "That's how they are."

"Yes, an Estonian," he repeated with that distant look again. "I think I know what you are talking about."

Erland and I are old pros when it comes to Estonian women. We both married Estonians, and so know them as intimately as foreigners can. Most foreigners seldom make it to this layer of deep knowledge that Erland and I have obtained. Instead these silly boys are still caught up in the vortex of their looks. "Oh, they are so beautiful!" "Oh, they are so sexy."

You can imagine how boring it gets for experts like us to hear young men chatter on about their sojourns to and from the nightclub with Triinu and Piret and Kaili. "There's just something about Signe," one once gushed to me. "I think I love her." How embarrassing. You just want to grab one of these Estonian-courting cads by the shirt and shake him.

"Don't you know?" you want to yell in his face. "Don't you have a clue what you are getting yourself into? Don't you know that soon your life will only consist of doing tedious home renovation jobs while your

Estonian true love sits on the computer all day long reading *Perekool*!"

But they don't listen. They are zombies, mesmerized by the grace of this northern species, just like Erland and I used to be. They have that distant look in their eyes, the look of men at sea. But since these guys haven't become the "proud owners" of an Estonian spouse yet, they are still hung up on those first impressions—the looks. They gaze at guys like Erland and me as if we had won the lottery, as if our wives were trophies. We are winners, they think, of the Bride Olympics.

They aren't all idiots. And I know where they get their ideas, because the Estonians gladly circulate the myth that they host the most beautiful women in the world. Just take a glance at *Kroonika*. It's a catalog of platinum blonde Barbies, usually straddling some kind of masculine-related item, a motorcycle perhaps, if not an actual man. A jaunt across Tallinn will leave a man feeling equally stimulated as he spies young ladies wearing the world's shortest skirts and hoop-earrings—a sure sign that they are ovulating and desperately want him!

These are the lures, the worms the Estonian ladies use to catch their fish. And like any good fisherwomen, when they tug them out of the water, like salmon from a flowing stream, they take out their metaphorical sticks and club the fish in the head until he is so dazed and so disoriented that he agrees to move to Estonia and start learning the Estonian language.

That's how the more industrious Estonian women operate. They look pretty, sure, they stand up straight, they are firm, but inside they are cold and hard and determined as *Peipsi* ice.

"So why do so many foreign men marry Estonian women?" my friend Janika asked me one night. Janika is an interior decorator who dabbles in the occult. She has been together with her American husband Scott since Lennart Meri was president. Apparently, she can't figure out what guys like Scott see in her and others like her. She's baffled. Why her? Why them?

I think I know why guys like us wound up married to Estonian women, but that's not what I said to Janika that night.

Instead I played the diplomat and told Janika that Estonians are not unique, that men are like bees, jumping from flower to flower, fulfilling the Fletcher Christian fantasy. Fletcher Christian was the first mate of the HMS Bounty. He led the famous mutiny that saw him and fellow sailors abandon their captain so that they could live a life of ease with nude Polynesian teenagers and coconut trees in the South Pacific.

We men are like Christian inside, all of us. We are rootless mariners and even if we don't wander in real life, we do in our dreams. Nobody really wants to know what a man is thinking. No one should know. It's too dangerous. If men were forthcoming with their thoughts, if they sought to fulfill each and every primordial urge, all of society would collapse. It would be like *Lord of the Flies* on a far grander scale, which is why we need women, desperately, to save us.

We men have scattered the Earth in search of these civilizing women. Some of us wound up in Estonia, but we have counterparts in Latvia and Finland, in Thailand and Argentina. Even Fletcher Christian's descendants are still in the South Pacific. So, I told Janika that night, you Estonians are not unique. These bicultural partnerships are going on all the time. It is the march of history. It cannot be stopped!

That being said, I told her that I think Estonians are amenable to marriage. They have a liberal, "Eh, what the heck?" approach to it and see it as a manifestation of romantic love, as opposed to the US where it has been viewed over the past few decades or so as a phase in life that occurs after a big promotion at work.

And, unlike in America, men in Estonia aren't expected to go to great lengths to make a proposal, like buying some exorbitantly priced ring or leaving a trail of candles across two counties that lead to the man who is waiting on his knees. Estonian women don't care about that stuff. Expensive rings are a waste of money. Elaborate displays of affection frighten them. These are women who maybe saw their father tell their mother he loved her one time. They don't expect that much.

So, in this context of ladies that aren't afraid to get married and wandering guys that are looking for a place to put down their roots, it shouldn't be surprising that so many foreign guys wash up on Estonian soil.

A final factor is that Estonia is 54 percent female and 46 percent male, and of that 46 percent, a good chunk are either drunks or Eurovision fans. That leaves the market wide open for international couplings.

That's was my official explanation to Janika, but it wasn't the truth. The truth was that I probably wound up with an Estonian woman because Estonian women are so terrifying. Think about it. Estonian women know how to survive in the forests, which berries are in season, what mushrooms are safe to eat, which trees are sacred, what moss will cure your cold. When Estonian women get sick, they wear necklaces of garlic and drink *nõiajook*, "witches' brew", a strange and yet restorative elixir. We can try and convince ourselves that they are just like American women or British women, but they are not. Estonian women are just different.

If an Estonian woman started to talk about how elves really exist and how she converses with them while she goes out mushrooming, telling her where the best chanterelles were to be found, I would probably believe her 100 percent, because why would she lie about a thing like that? You know how they are. They are firm, straight-backed, austere, serious and sober. They don't make jokes about things like that. Do they?

This has led me to wonder if fellows like me and Erland and Scott are really here of our own free will, or if the women in our lives merely slipped some mixture of wild herbs into our drinks. But, at this stage, how we got here doesn't matter. We were once wild salmon swimming upstream. Then the hot-blooded Estonian fisherwomen hooked us and pulled us out of the water and very firmly clubbed us on the heads. Now we tinker around with home renovation projects while our wives read *Perekool*. The end.

Thank You!

I still don't know who gave me the chocolate. She never introduced herself. After the line of readers seeking autographs at the bookstore in Tallinn was exhausted, she approached me and handed me the large Geisha bar. She was about half my height, young, blonde, female, reserved; in a word, an Estonian.

"Here," she said, handing me the chocolate, her voice trembling slightly. "This is for you." I took the chocolate and thanked her, and then she said, "OK," and ran away.

"It's not bad to be famous!" remarked my wife's Aunt Reeli, who stood nearby. "Not bad at all." Reeli had brought me a Tuborg beer as a gift. Only later, I recalled that I had written about Geisha chocolate and Tuborg beer in my books and so their gifts were quite meaningful. But that was only later; at the time, it all seemed quite random.

Was I really famous, like Reeli had said? I didn't think so, but my daughter's 10-year old friend Kaisi seemed to think I knew something about fame. "I've read that famous people actually don't like being famous," she said as she waited for me while I signed the last books. We were preparing for the drive back to Viljandi, where my daughters were preparing for a slumber party. "I've read that famous people can't walk down the street without people taking their pictures," Kaisi said. "Has that happened to you?"

"I'm not that famous, Kaisi," I told her. Still, my perception of fame has changed. I recall how I had approached the esteemed British journalist Edward Lucas several years ago at a conference in Tallinn seeking an autograph for his book, *The New Cold War*. As soon as I saw Edward I started to sweat. Here was the man who had written a great tome on geopolitics in the flesh! I tripped twice as I walked towards him. My hands shook as I held his book out, upside down, for him to sign it. But Edward seemed unfazed. He turned the book around, signed it, and handed it back, all with a leisurely smile. Edward was used to it. He has been meeting clumsy readers for years.

Now it's my turn in the author's seat. I've seen people trip on their way to speak to me, watched their hands shake as they hand the books over for me to sign. Why do their hands shake? I just don't know, but I guess it can happen to anyone. It's taken about a year, but, like Lucas, I have become accustomed to this new phenomenon of shaking shaky hands. And readers don't just want my autograph, they want to give things. In addition to chocolates and beer, I've been blessed with other gifts: flowers, cards, books, DVDs, blueberries. People ask if they can hug me, or if they can have their photo taken with me, to which I am happy to oblige. Someone even gave me a painted ceramic frog. It now sits on my shelf alongside the half-eaten Geisha chocolate.

And then there are the questions. Some are more typical. "Do you write in Estonian?" "Do you speak to your children in Estonian?" "The Estonian language is hard, isn't it?" "Have you tried *sült* yet?" But then there are the more unique queries. "Are Estonians intolerant?" "What do you think about the euro?" "Can you write something so that my daughter will finally move back from the United States?" Sometimes things get too personal. "Do you live in *that* house?" "Does your daughter go to *that* school?" "Can we come visit you?"

Once a reader, who also was the sister of a friend, really did come back to our apartment, where we discussed the content of my latest column. "You know the one you wrote about the woman who was having an affair with the Colombian drug dealer?" "Uh huh," I nodded. "I have a lot of friends who fantasize about something like that happening to them," she confessed. "It sounds so sexy." And so I gained new insight into the psyche of Estonian women. But that's what I enjoy most about meeting with readers.

It's also reassuring to meet people who think you've done something right. I say this because, like most artists, I am tortured by my own work. Everything I write could have been better. Nothing was ever good enough. Here I am reminded of Rivers Cuomo, the lead singer of the rock band Weezer, who upon learning that the band's first album went platinum promptly fell into depression, painted all the walls of his room black, and refused to touch his guitar or talk to his bandmates (he was later coaxed out of his black room and has since written many other good songs).

It's the readers who have convinced me to write more. One of them, an older lady, pulled me aside the other day at a bookstore. "Do you thank the heavens that you can write?" she asked. "The heavens?" I said, confused. "You mean the clouds?" "Yes, you have been given a gift," the old woman said. "Not everyone can write. So, you should thank the heavens for your ability." "Alright," I said. "I'll do that." And when I got outside the store, I looked up at the milky gray Estonian skies, and thanked them.